Anger Transformed: Embracing God's Grace for Emotional Well-being

Andrew J. Lamont-Turner

Published by Andrew J. Lamont-Turner, 2024.

ANGER TRANSFORMED: EMBRACING GOD'S GRACE FOR EMOTIONAL WELL-BEING

First edition. April 6, 2024.

ISBN: 979-8224290352

Written by Andrew J. Lamont-Turner.

Table of Contents

Anger Transformed
Embracing God's Grace for Emotional Well-being

Copyright Andrew J Lamont-Turner 2023
First Edition: 2023

Scripture quotations marked CSB have been taken from the Christian Standard Bible®, Copyright © 2017 by Holman Bible Publishers. Used by permission. Christian Standard Bible® and CSB® are federally registered trademarks of Holman Bible Publishers.

Scripture quotations marked ESV are from the ESV® Bible (The Holy Bible, English Standard Version®), copyright © 2001 by Crossway Bibles, a publishing ministry of Good News Publishers. Used by permission. All rights reserved.

Scripture quotations marked NKJV are taken from the New King James Version. Copyright © 1982 by Thomas Nelson, Inc. Used by permission. All rights reserved.

Scripture quotations marked WEB are taken from the World English Bible. Public Domain.

Cover Page Design by AJ Lamont-Turner

1. Introduction

In this introductory chapter, we embark on a journey to explore the intricate realm of anger management through the lens of biblical wisdom. The purpose of this book is to provide guidance and support for individuals seeking to understand, control, and transform their anger in a way that aligns with the teachings of the Bible.

The Relevance of Biblical Principles in Anger Management: Anger is a universal emotion experienced by individuals from all walks of life. It can arise from various triggers, such as personal frustrations, conflicts, or perceived injustices. Recognising the relevance of biblical principles in anger management, we explore the wisdom and insights the Scriptures offer to navigate this complex emotion. By exploring the intersections of faith and anger, we aim to uncover practical strategies rooted in biblical teachings that can help individuals harness their anger constructively and restore harmony in their lives.

Benefits of Applying Biblical Wisdom: Applying biblical wisdom in the context of anger management offers profound benefits for individuals striving to achieve emotional well-being, healthier relationships, and spiritual growth. Throughout this book, we will explore the transformative power of biblical principles and their potential to reshape our understanding and response to anger. Exploring these teachings opens doors to enhanced self-awareness, emotional resilience, forgiveness, and a deeper connection with God.

As we embark on this journey, let us approach the topic of anger management with an open heart and mind, ready to embrace the wisdom of the Bible and the transformative possibilities it holds. Together, we will navigate the complexities of anger, uncover strategies for managing it effectively, and discover a path towards inner peace and spiritual growth.

Prayer

Dear Heavenly Father,

We come before You with hearts filled with gratitude and reverence, recognising Your unwavering love and guidance in our lives. As we embark on this journey of exploring the depths of our emotions, specifically anger, we humbly seek Your presence and wisdom to illuminate our path.

Lord, we acknowledge that anger is a natural human emotion. Still, we recognise that it can have detrimental effects if left unchecked. We acknowledge the need for self-reflection and introspection to understand the root causes of our anger and how it may affect our lives and relationships.

Father, as we explore this chapter's contents, we pray for open hearts and receptive minds. Help us to grasp the importance of managing our anger in a way that aligns with Your principles. Teach us to discern between righteous anger and uncontrolled rage, guiding us to respond in ways that reflect Your character.

Grant us the humility to recognise and courage to confront our weaknesses. May we surrender our pride and allow Your transformative power to work within us. Help us to release any bitterness or resentment that may have taken root in our hearts, replacing it with forgiveness and compassion.

Lord, we acknowledge that true change can only come through Your grace and the work of Your Holy Spirit. We humbly submit ourselves to You, asking for the strength and perseverance to walk this anger management journey. Help us to lean on Your promises and to trust in Your sovereignty, knowing that You are faithful to guide us through every challenge.

As we reflect on the contents of this chapter, may we be empowered to seek reconciliation and restoration in our relationships. May grace and humility mark our words and actions, and may we strive to build a world of peace, love, and unity.

We thank You, Lord, for your wisdom and guidance through Your Word. May the lessons learned from this chapter not simply remain knowledge, but may they be translated into tangible transformation in our lives.

In Jesus' name, we pray.

Amen.

1.1 Purpose of the book

This book aims to provide individuals with biblical principles for managing their anger. It aims to offer helpful guidance and support for those looking to comprehend, manage, and transform their anger in a way that complies with biblical teachings.

People naturally experience anger in various circumstances, but if it is not controlled, it can cause problems. The Bible acknowledges the existence of anger and guides how to manage it to foster interpersonal harmony, emotional health, and personal development.

The understanding that God's Word offers instruction for all areas of life, including our emotions, is the foundation for the applicability of biblical principles in anger management. The Bible teaches us about the nature of anger, its possible effects, and how to deal with it in a way that is under God's will.

Examining the biblical definition of anger is a crucial step in comprehending anger from a biblical perspective. According to Ephesians 4:26, the Bible recognises that anger may be a proper reaction to wrongdoing or injustice. But it also issues a warning against irrational and destructive rage (Proverbs 29:11). We can learn about the various manifestations and effects of anger by looking at biblical examples, such as Moses' anger in Exodus 32:19–20 or Jesus' righteous anger in Mark 11:15–17.

God's perspective on anger is complex. The Bible emphasises God's patience, love, and mercy while acknowledging that He can become angry (Exodus 34:6–7; Psalm 145:8–9). Since we were made in God's likeness, we must emulate Him in all our thoughts, feelings, and deeds, even when we are angry. The Bible exhorts us to avoid holding grudges and resentments by encouraging us to be slow to anger (James 1:19-20) and to seek peace and forgiveness (Matthew 5:23-24, Colossians 3:13).

Uncontrolled anger can negatively affect one's health, relationships, and spiritual life. Proverbs 15:1 and Proverbs 29:22 both forewarn against the negative outcomes of anger, including strife, division, and hurtful words. Understanding these repercussions can help people become more motivated to pursue biblically-based anger management.

The key to controlling your anger is to seek God's direction. To control anger effectively, prayer and asking for divine guidance are essential. The Bible exhorts us to bring our worries and feelings before God (Philippians 4:6-7) and to ask for His direction in every area of life, including controlling our rage. Angry people can find strength, peace, and clarity through prayer, allowing God's transforming power to work in their lives.

Studying pertinent verses from the Bible is another essential component of seeking God's direction for anger control. The Bible contains a wealth of lessons and parables that shed light on anger and how to control it. Proverbs 14:29, Galatians 5:22–23, and Ephesians 4:31–32, for example, offer guidance on cultivating virtues like self-control, patience, forgiveness, and love, which are crucial in biblically managing anger.

Anger management starts with forging a close relationship with God. People can experience change in their attitudes, thoughts, and behaviours related to anger by developing a close relationship with God through consistent Bible study, prayer, and fellowship with other believers. The Bible teaches that God wants a close, personal relationship with each person and that through this relationship, He can give people the wisdom, courage, and grace they need to control their anger.

The biblical guidelines for controlling your anger cover many facets of life. Scripture strongly emphasises self-control (Proverbs 25:28; Galatians 5:23). It entails developing self-control over one's feelings and behaviour so that people can react to anger in a measured and controlled way. It is necessary to rely on the power of the Holy Spirit and align one's desires with God's will to develop self-control.

A crucial aspect of controlling anger is forgiveness. According to the Bible (Ephesians 4:32; Colossians 3:13), Christians are to show mercy to one another as God has shown them mercy. People can free themselves from the weight of anger by choosing forgiveness over holding on to grudges, and they can also experience emotional healing and the restoration of their relationships.

Meekness and humility are virtues that temper anger's destructive tendencies. The Bible (James 4:6, Matthew 5:5) exhorts people to develop a humble and gentle spirit while acknowledging their limitations and weaknesses. Instead of retaliating in rage, humble people can approach situations with a willingness to listen, understand, and come to an amicable agreement.

Biblical anger management requires the virtues of patience and endurance. According to the Bible, love is patient (1 Corinthians 13:4). That patience is a fruit of the Spirit (Galatians 5:22). When faced with difficult situations, patience involves exercising restraint and endurance, giving things time to work out and grow rather than reacting indignantly right away.

From a biblical perspective, the fundamental principles that govern effective anger management are love and compassion. The Bible exhorts believers to show compassion and empathy for others (Ephesians 4:32). It emphasises the value of love in all relationships (1 Corinthians 13:4–7). People can respond to anger with understanding and seek reconciliation rather than retaliation by practising love and compassion.

An essential component of anger control is the application of biblical wisdom to conflict resolution. The Bible offers instruction on communication, stressing the value of speaking the truth in love (Ephesians 4:15) and peacefully resolving disputes (Matthew 18:15–17). By adhering to these guidelines, people can encourage constructive conversation, look for peace, and mend relations that have been damaged.

Biblical teachings strongly emphasise controlling anger through faith and trust in God. People can release their anger to God by trusting His plan and sovereignty and relying on His strength and direction (Proverbs 3:5–6). Even in situations that might make them angry, people can find solace, peace, and assurance by cultivating their faith and trust in God.

Biblical advice on managing anger emphasises restorative justice and forgiveness. (Micah 6:8, Matthew 6:14–15) The Bible emphasises the values of justice grounded in mercy and forgiveness. Through restorative justice, people aim to promote their own healing, the healing of broken relationships, and the chance for others to experience transformation and forgiveness.

Beyond singular incidents, anger management affects all aspects of daily life. A consistent commitment to live by God's Word is necessary to apply biblical principles to everyday challenges. It entails channelling rage into positive actions like arguing for justice, resisting oppression, and encouraging reconciliation. People who live a life of peace, restraint, and obedience to God's commands can better control their anger in all facets of their lives.

Through this book, users are given the tools they need to deal with their anger in a way that fosters spiritual well-being, healthy relationships, and personal development. The chapter emphasises the significance of understanding the biblical viewpoint on anger, including its definition, effects, and God's perspective. It emphasises the importance of seeking God's direction through prayer, Bible study, and cultivating a close relationship with Him.

The chapter discusses using biblical wisdom in conflict resolution and other important biblical principles for controlling anger, such as self-control, forgiveness, humility, patience, and love. It emphasises the role of restorative justice and forgiveness in healing and reconciliation and the transformative power of faith and trust in God. The chapter ends by emphasising how biblical principles can be applied to daily life and exhorting readers to develop a way of life characterised by tranquillity, restraint, and obedience to God's commands.

Readers can embark on a journey of self-reflection, growth, and transformation in managing anger by engaging with the teachings and principles outlined in this book. The subsequent chapters explore each subject, offering helpful tips, biblical illustrations, and direction on effectively implementing these principles. People can experience the transforming power of controlling anger in a way that honours God and promotes personal and relational flourishing by faithfully studying the Scriptures and being willing to accept their lessons.

Questions for Reflection

What is my personal motivation for seeking to understand and manage my anger?

Am I genuinely committed to personal growth and positive change in this area of my life?

How does this book's purpose align with my goals and aspirations for improving my anger management skills?

What specific outcomes do I hope to achieve through reading and applying the principles shared in this book?

1.2 The Relevance of biblical principles in anger management

Anger is a common human emotion that can harm people on many levels, including their relationships, relationships, and general quality of life. Examining how biblical principles can direct people towards healthy and helpful ways of managing their anger is crucial in anger management. The importance of incorporating biblical wisdom into managing anger is explored in this chapter, which also highlights the profound insights and useful applications that can be drawn from the Scriptures.

Due to their ageless wisdom and divine direction, biblical principles have a special relevance in anger management. The teachings, stories, and examples found in the Bible offer deep insights into human nature, emotions, and interpersonal relationships. People can develop a comprehensive understanding of anger and discover how to deal with this difficult emotion consistent with God's plan for human flourishing by drawing on the Scriptures.

The emphasis biblical principles place on addressing the underlying causes of anger rather than just treating its symptoms is one of the main reasons they apply to anger management. The Bible recognises that various things, including unmet expectations, injustice, and personal wounds, can give rise to anger. People can learn more about the underlying issues that fuel their anger and find constructive ways to deal with them by studying biblical passages.

Biblical principles also provide a thorough framework for comprehending the nature of anger and its effects. The Bible offers a balanced view of anger, acknowledging its potential for harm and that it can occasionally be a justified reaction to wrongdoing or injustice. Ephesians 4:26–27, for example, warns, "In your anger, do not sin: Do not let the sun go down while you are still angry, and do not give the devil a foothold." This verse emphasises how critical it is to recognise your anger and deal with it immediately to limit its negative effects.

Biblical principles also offer advice on how to cultivate virtues that are crucial for efficient anger management. Proverbs 14:29 says, "Whoever is slow to anger has great understanding, but he who has a hasty temper exalts folly." The importance of self-control and patience in controlling anger is emphasised in this verse. By cultivating these virtues, people can learn to control their anger and respond to it in a helpful way rather than impulsively or destructively.

Biblical principles' applicability to anger management also stems from their capacity to foster spiritual transformation and development. The Scriptures emphasise how the indwelling of the Holy Spirit and God's grace can transform people, enabling them to overcome destructive patterns of anger and cultivate virtues like love, forgiveness, and compassion. Romans 12:2 exhorts Christians to be transformed by renewing their minds, showing that anger management involves changing one's behaviour and undergoing inner renewal because of a personal relationship with God.

Individuals are encouraged to adopt a holistic strategy that addresses their spiritual, emotional, and relational well-being by incorporating biblical principles into anger management. The Bible contains many instructions on controlling your anger in ways consistent with God's character and purposes. James 1:19–20, for instance, says, "My dear brothers and sisters, take note of this: Everyone should be quick to listen, slow to speak, and slow to become angry because human anger does not produce the righteousness that God desires." This verse emphasises thoughtful communication, active listening, and self-control as crucial anger management elements reflecting God's righteousness.

Biblical principles apply to forgiveness, reconciliation, and anger management. The Bible emphasises forgiveness as a powerfully transformative and healing action. Christians are urged to "Bear with each other and forgive one another if any of you has a grievance against someone," according to Colossians 3:13. As the Lord forgave you, forgive others. This verse emphasises that forgiveness is important in resolving disputes and mending damaged relationships. People can experience freedom from the weight of resentment and progress towards reconciliation and restoration by practising biblical forgiveness.

The importance of biblical principles for controlling anger cannot be overstated. The Scriptures provide profound understanding, useful instruction, and transformative wisdom for comprehending and successfully controlling anger. By studying the Bible's teachings, people can gain a comprehensive understanding of anger, pinpoint the causes of their anger, cultivate virtues like self-control and patience, and accept forgiveness and reconciliation as transformative practices. The Bible offers a timeless and priceless resource for those looking to navigate the complexities of anger in a way that aligns with God's will and fosters personal development and relational well-being.

People are encouraged to seek a closer relationship with God, develop virtues that reflect His character, and rely on the power of the Holy Spirit for transformation as they interact with biblical principles in anger management. People can experience healing, restoration, and the emergence of healthier thoughts, emotions, and behaviour patterns by grounding their anger management journey in biblical wisdom.

It's crucial to understand that there is no one-size-fits-all method for managing anger when using biblical principles. Each person's journey will be different, and seeking advice from reputable spiritual mentors, counsellors, and faith communities can offer extra support and insights.

People can access a source of knowledge and direction that cuts across time and cultural contexts by accepting the relevance of biblical principles in anger management. The Bible offers a strong foundation for comprehending anger, overcoming its difficulties, and going through a personal and relational transformation. People can find healing, peace, and restoration as they travel towards a life marked by emotional health, wholesome relationships, and alignment with God's purposes through prayer, Bible study, and reliance on God's grace.

Questions for Reflection

How can biblical principles enhance and inform my approach to anger management?

How does integrating biblical wisdom into my strategies and techniques contribute to a more holistic and effective approach?

How have my previous attempts at anger management been influenced or limited by a lack of consideration for biblical principles?

What insights can I gain from exploring the relevance of biblical principles in this area of my life?

1.3 Benefits of Applying Biblical Wisdom

The advantages of using biblical wisdom in anger control are numerous and far-reaching. Individuals can experience a revolutionary change in their emotional well-being, relationships, and overall quality of life by embracing the applicability of biblical ideas. The Scriptures provide excellent insights and direction for biblically understanding anger and providing practical knowledge for handling it healthily and constructively.

Aligning with God's will is one of the key benefits of using biblical wisdom in anger management. The Bible is a divine instruction manual for navigating the intricacies of human emotions, especially rage. According to Proverbs 14:29, a patient demonstrates great insight, but a quick-tempered person fosters stupidity. Individuals can connect their responses to anger with God's plans for their lives by following biblical principles.

Biblical wisdom encourages self-awareness and contemplation. In times of rage, the Scriptures exhort people to examine their hearts and reasons. "Search me, God, and know my heart; test me, and know my anxious thoughts," Psalm 139:23-24 begs. See if there is any offensive way in me, and eternally lead me. Individuals can obtain insights into their anger triggers, underlying difficulties, and unproductive thought patterns by applying biblical wisdom, leading to personal growth and emotional maturity.

Using biblical understanding to handle anger promotes good relationships. The Bible instructs us to successfully communicate, resolve disagreements, and treat others with love and respect. According to Proverbs 15:1, "A gentle answer turns away wrath, but a harsh word stirs up anger." Individuals who embrace this philosophy can de-escalate unpleasant situations, enhance understanding, and develop happy relationships.

Biblical teaching stresses the importance of forgiveness and reconciliation as vital components of anger management. "Get rid of all bitterness, rage and anger, brawling and slander, as well as every form of malice," Ephesians 4:31-32 urges. Be kind and sympathetic to one another, forgiving one another as God has forgiven you in Christ." Individuals can release grudges, let go of resentment, and experience the healing power of forgiveness by following this counsel, leading to repaired relationships and emotional liberation.

The use of biblical wisdom in anger management has spiritual benefits as well. Individuals can achieve spiritual growth and transformation by seeking God's guidance and depending on His strength. According to James 1:19, "Everyone should be quick to listen, slow to speak, and slow to become angry." This verse encourages people to acquire patience, self-control, and humility, leading to a stronger relationship with God and a better fit with His character.

Using biblical wisdom to regulate anger fosters inner peace and emotional well-being. Philippians 4:6-7 encourages people to give thanks for their petitions to God, and the peace of God, which surpasses all understanding, will protect their hearts and minds in Christ Jesus. Individuals who commit their fury to God might experience serenity beyond human comprehension, finding refuge and emotional stability in difficult situations.

It is crucial to highlight that the advantages of using biblical wisdom in anger control are not immediate or automatic. They necessitate deliberate work, humility, and reliance on God's grace. Individuals can gradually experience the transformational benefits of biblical wisdom in managing their anger by constantly seeking God's guidance, studying His Word, and following His precepts.

The advantages of using biblical wisdom in anger control are numerous and significant. Individuals can experience life change by aligning with God's will, achieving self-awareness, nurturing healthy relationships, embracing forgiveness, experiencing spiritual growth, and cultivating inner peace.

Individuals can comprehend anger from a biblical viewpoint and learn how to manage it in a way that honours God and promotes personal well-being by applying biblical principles. The Scriptures offer direction and practical insight that may be applied in everyday life, assisting individuals in navigating their emotions, responding to conflict, and fostering good relationships.

Individuals can develop a greater awareness of their hearts and reasons by embracing biblical principles, allowing them to handle anger at its fundamental causes. This self-awareness allows people to mature emotionally, resulting in healthier displays of rage and a stronger sense of inner calm.

Using biblical understanding in anger management improves relationships. The Bible's teachings on love, forgiveness, and reconciliation provide a foundation for resolving disagreements and rebuilding damaged connections. Individuals can create healthier and more meaningful relationships with others by adhering to these guidelines.

Using biblical wisdom in anger management spiritually empowers people to live by God's purposes and wants. It entails seeking God's guidance, relying on His strength, and giving over one's anger to Him. Individuals can experience spiritual growth, strengthen their relationship with God, and find comfort and tranquillity in His presence.

The advantages of using biblical wisdom in anger control go beyond the person. Individuals who learn to regulate their anger healthily and productively help make their community more peaceful and harmonious. By exemplifying forgiveness, compassion, and patience, they motivate others to do the same, resulting in a positive ripple effect.

It is vital to highlight that using biblical wisdom in anger management is a lifelong process that necessitates patience and reliance on God's love. It includes frequent Bible study, prayer, and seeking instruction from the Holy Spirit. Individuals who commit to continuously adopting biblical principles will experience the transformative impact of God's Word in their lives.

Finally, the advantages of using biblical wisdom in anger control are substantial. They include personal development, healthy relationships, spiritual progress, and contributing to a more peaceful community. We can negotiate anger with wisdom, kindness, and humility by accepting the applicability of biblical concepts and integrating them into our lives, ultimately experiencing the transformative power of God's Word in our journey towards emotional well-being and spiritual development.

Questions for Reflection

What benefits do I anticipate experiencing by applying biblical wisdom to my anger management journey?

How do I envision these benefits positively impacting my well-being, relationships, and spiritual growth?

In what ways have I seen or experienced the positive effects of biblical principles in other areas of my life?

How can I leverage those experiences and insights to better understand the benefits of applying biblical wisdom to anger management?

2. Understanding Anger from a Biblical Perspective

Anger is a universal human emotion we all experience at various times. It is a powerful force that, if not properly managed, can harm our well-being, relationships, and overall spiritual growth. This chapter will explore anger from a biblical perspective, seeking wisdom and guidance from the Scriptures to better understand its nature, causes, and potential consequences.

Anger, in its essence, is an emotional response to perceived wrongdoing, injustice, or a threat to our well-being. It can manifest in various forms, from mild irritation to intense rage. While anger itself is not inherently sinful, it is crucial to recognise that it has the potential to lead to sin if left unchecked or expressed in destructive ways. The Bible provides valuable insights into the nature of anger and its potential impact on our lives.

Throughout the Scriptures, we find numerous accounts of individuals who experienced and expressed anger. From righteous indignation to uncontrolled wrath, these examples serve as valuable lessons for us to understand the complexities of anger and its consequences. We will explore biblical stories such as Moses' anger at the Israelites' disobedience, David's righteous anger at Goliath's blasphemy, and Jesus' righteous anger at religious hypocrisy.

As we seek to understand anger from a biblical perspective, we must examine God's view on this powerful emotion. While the Bible acknowledges the existence of anger, it also guides how to manage and channel it righteously. We will explore passages that reveal God's perspective on anger, including His admonitions to be slow to anger, to avoid sinning in our anger, and to seek reconciliation rather than harbouring resentment.

Uncontrolled anger can profoundly affect our well-being, relationships, and spiritual life. The Scriptures warn us about the destructive effects of anger and urge us to exercise self-control in managing our emotions. We will explore the potential physical, emotional, and relational repercussions of uncontrolled anger, highlighting the importance of addressing this issue.

Recognising the potential pitfalls of anger, the Bible guides us on effectively managing this powerful emotion. We will explore practical steps for seeking God's guidance in anger management, including the role of prayer, studying relevant biblical passages, and developing a personal relationship with God that allows His transformative power to work within us.

In the subsequent chapters, we will deeply explore biblical principles and practical daily strategies for managing anger. By aligning our understanding of anger with biblical wisdom, we can cultivate emotional maturity, foster healthy relationships, and experience spiritual growth.

Understanding anger from a biblical perspective is essential for personal growth and spiritual development. As we explore the nature of anger, examine biblical examples, and discern God's view on this emotion, we gain insights that will help us navigate the complexities of anger in a manner that honours God and promotes well-being. The following chapters will explore the practical application of biblical principles for anger management. We will equip ourselves with the tools to transform anger into constructive action and cultivate a life marked by peace, love, and self-control.

Prayer

Heavenly Father,

We come before You with grateful hearts, recognising that You are the source of all wisdom and understanding. As we explore this chapter's contents, we humbly seek Your guidance and illumination to comprehend anger from a biblical perspective.

Lord, we acknowledge that anger is a complex emotion that can motivate positive action and lead to destructive consequences. Help us to discern the difference between righteous anger that aligns with Your truth and uncontrolled anger that stems from selfishness and pride.

This chapter explores how anger can impact our lives and relationships. We ask Your grace to bring clarity and self-awareness as we examine our hearts and behaviours. May Your Spirit reveal any unresolved anger or hurt that may be hindering our growth and causing harm to ourselves and others.

Father, we recognise that You are a God of justice and righteousness. Help us to understand how to navigate our anger in a way that aligns with Your character. Teach us to seek peaceful resolutions and approach conflicts with humility and grace. May we learn to respond to provocation with love and understanding, reflecting the transformative power of Your Word in our lives.

Lord, we acknowledge that true change begins with surrendering our hearts to You. Help us release any bitterness, resentment, or unforgiveness that may have taken root. Fill us with Your peace and grant us the strength to extend forgiveness to those who have wronged us, just as You have forgiven us.

As we explore the biblical principles surrounding anger, we ask for Your divine wisdom to guide our thoughts and actions. May the lessons learned in this chapter deepen our understanding of Your truth and transform us into vessels of Your love and reconciliation.

Father, we commit ourselves to the ongoing process of self-reflection and growth. Grant us the courage to confront our shortcomings and the willingness to seek reconciliation and healing in our relationships. May Your grace empower us to overcome anger and walk in righteousness.

We thank You, Lord, for the wisdom and insight You have provided through Your Word. May the lessons learned from this chapter not be mere intellectual knowledge, but may they shape our hearts and lead us to a life that reflects Your love, mercy, and grace.

In Jesus' name, we pray.

Amen.

2.1 The Nature of Anger

Anger is a complex and varied emotion that has existed in the human experience since humanity's dawn. It is a natural reaction to events that endanger our well-being, challenge our ideals, or violate our rights. To understand rage from a biblical standpoint, we must first examine its nature and traits.

The Bible recognises the reality of rage and offers significant insights into its different manifestations. The apostle Paul states in Ephesians 4:26, "Be angry and do not sin; do not let the sun go down on your anger." This verse implies that anger is not intrinsically immoral. A natural human emotion can push us to rectify injustices or confront wrongdoing. However, Paul warns against allowing wrath to fester, which can lead to immoral thoughts, words, and acts.

According to Proverbs 14:29, "Whoever is slow to anger has great understanding, but he who has a hasty temper exalts folly." This passage emphasises the need for self-control and not letting emotions rule our reactions. It emphasises the wisdom of being patient and measured in our reactions rather than rashly. This is consistent with the larger biblical idea of self-control as a fruit of the Spirit (Galatians 5:22-23), emphasising the need to manage our emotions in a way that honours God.

It is critical to recognise that unrestrained anger can rapidly turn into sin. In His Sermon on the Mount, Jesus stated, "But I say to you that everyone angry with his brother will be liable to judgement; whoever insults his brother will be liable to the council; and whoever says, 'You fool!' will be liable to the hell of fire" (Matthew 5:22). In this passage, Jesus emphasises the importance of addressing not only the outward manifestations of anger but also the attitudes and thoughts that give rise to it. He exhorts His followers to seek reconciliation and to avoid harbouring ill will towards others.

Understanding the potential risks of unbridled wrath requires acknowledging that the Bible contains examples of righteous indignation. In John 2:13-16, we see Jesus exhibiting righteous rage by overturning the money changers' tables in the temple. This chapter demonstrates that there are times when anger is reasonable and appropriate, especially when it is used to redress injustice or maintain the integrity of God's sanctuary.

Even in moments of righteous rage, the Bible exhorts believers to be cautious. "Know this, my beloved brothers: let everyone be quick to hear, slow to speak, and slow to anger; for man's anger does not produce God's righteousness," James 1:19-20 says. This verse reminds us that, even if we feel justified in our wrath, we must be careful of our reactions and strive to line them with God's justice. It exhorts us to listen quickly and slowly to wrath, acknowledging that human anger cannot bring about the righteousness that God seeks.

The Bible depicts the essence of wrath as varied and subtle. It accepts that anger is a natural human emotion but warns that it can lead to sin if not managed properly. Instead of allowing anger to fester and escalate, the Scriptures encourage self-control, patience, and a readiness to seek reconciliation. They also give examples of righteous wrath and emphasise the importance of aligning our reactions with God's righteousness. We can gain a deeper knowledge of anger from a biblical viewpoint and learn how to navigate this emotion to please God by studying these biblical principles.

As we continue our biblical investigation of anger management, the following chapters will investigate numerous facets of anger, its ramifications, and practical techniques for dealing with it per biblical principles. We will investigate the negative impacts of uncontrollable rage on personal well-being, relationships, and spiritual development. We will also examine how prayer, seeking divine wisdom, and studying pertinent biblical scriptures can help us seek God's assistance in managing anger.

We will look at biblical ideas that can help us manage our anger properly. These principles include developing self-control and the fruit of the Spirit, forgiving and letting go of resentment, adopting humility and meekness, growing patience and long-suffering, and exhibiting love and compassion towards others.

We will look at how to use biblical wisdom in dispute resolution, focusing on biblically directed communication, pursuing reconciliation and peace-making, and responding to provocation with grace. We'll also examine how faith and trust can help you overcome anger, develop resilience, and rely on God's purpose and sovereignty.

We will look at restorative justice and forgiveness, biblical ideas of justice and the role of forgiveness in healing and reconciliation. In controlling anger and restoring relationships, we will discuss the significance of seeking restoration and making amends.

We will discuss applying anger management ideas in everyday life, such as dealing with daily challenges and channelling anger into positive activity. We will investigate the value of cultivating a peaceful and self-control lifestyle by aligning our ideas, words, and actions with biblical principles.

The final chapter will summarise significant biblical principles on anger control, encouraging personal growth and transformation. We will also provide other resources for additional biblical study, enabling readers to continue their path towards understanding and managing anger in a way consistent with God's Word.

We can acquire useful insights and practical assistance for handling anger in a way that honours God and promotes good relationships by diving into the rich knowledge of the Scriptures. Throughout this book, we will look at the transformative potential of biblical concepts and how they apply to anger management. Let us open our hearts and minds to the knowledge of God's Word as we embark on this journey together and strive to nurture a spirit of self-control, peace, and love in all our relationships.

May this biblical investigation of anger management equip and motivate us to live by God's instructions, encouraging reconciliation and cultivating emotional well-being in our lives and those around us.

Questions for Reflection

How does my understanding of the nature of anger align with the biblical perspective presented in Chapter 2.1?

How can I apply this understanding to my experiences and anger responses?

In what ways can I distinguish between righteous anger and uncontrolled, destructive anger in my own life?

How can I ensure that my anger is guided by biblical principles and used constructively for the glory of God?

2.2 Biblical definition of anger

The biblical definition of anger is a multidimensional notion that may be examined from numerous angles throughout the Bible. Anger, as represented in the Bible, encompasses a wide spectrum of emotions, attitudes, and behaviours. This discussion will examine the biblical concept of rage and its expressions, causes, and potential consequences.

Anger is often alluded to in the Bible by numerous names, such as wrath, indignation, rage, or burning displeasure. These words imply extreme emotion and the stimulation of a passionate reaction to a perceived offence or transgression. While anger is not necessarily immoral, understanding how the Bible distinguishes between righteous and unrighteous anger is critical.

Righteous fury, or holy or justified anger, is under God's nature and intentions. It is a fitting reaction to injustice, wrongdoing, or disobedience to God's commands. We discover examples of righteous anger shown by God, Jesus, and others throughout the Bible.

In the life of Jesus, one significant example of righteous indignation may be found. In the Gospels, Jesus showed his rage at religious leaders who exploited the poor and abused the Temple for personal gain (Matthew 21:12-13). This outburst of rage emphasises the significance of justice, compassion, and keeping God's rules.

The Bible, on the other hand, warns against wicked anger, which includes self-centeredness, hatred, and a desire for vengeance. Scripture warns against the devastating repercussions of unbridled wrath in various chapters. Proverbs 29:22, for example, warns that "an angry person stirs up conflict, and a hot-tempered person commits many sins." In Ephesians 4:26-27, the apostle Paul also warns, "In your anger do not sin: Do not let the sun go down while you are still angry, and do not give the devil a foothold."

The biblical definition of rage emphasises the value of self-control as well. According to Proverbs 16:32, "Better a patient person than a warrior, one with self-control than one who takes a city." This poem emphasises the need to control one's anger. It demonstrates that true strength comes from exercising self-discipline and intelligence.

The Bible admits that rage can quickly escalate to sinful behaviours such as verbal or physical abuse, resentment, and bitterness. In the Sermon on the Mount, Jesus compares harbouring anger and insulting others to the possibility of suffering judgment (Matthew 5:21-22). This teaching emphasises the importance of dealing with and resolving anger virtuously and constructively.

To completely comprehend the biblical concept of rage, it is necessary to analyse the underlying reasons for anger. While anger can be triggered by various events, the Bible lists several core causes, including pride, injustice, unmet expectations, and personal offences. According to James 1:19-20, "My dear brothers and sisters, take note of this: Everyone should be quick to listen, slow to speak, and slow to become angry because human anger does not produce the righteousness that God desires." In dealing with wrath, this chapter emphasises the value of humility, patience, and careful discernment.

Believers are called to seek transformation via the power of the Holy Spirit in dealing with anger biblically. The fruit of the Spirit is described in Galatians 5:22-23 as love, joy, peace, patience, kindness, goodness, faithfulness, gentleness, and self-control. As believers allow the Holy Spirit to work in their lives, these characteristics emerge, suppressing unjustified wrath and promoting godly reactions.

The biblical notion of anger includes both righteous and unjustified emotions. Righteous wrath is a response consistent with God's character and purposes, acting as a just and passionate reaction to injustice, evil, or disobedience. Unrighteous wrath, conversely, is characterised by self-centeredness and a desire for vengeance, which can result in negative repercussions and immoral deeds.

According to the biblical understanding of rage, true power exerts restraint and wisdom. The Bible cautions against the harmful effects of excessive anger. It encourages believers to handle and resolve their anger righteously and constructively. The root reasons for anger, such as pride, injustice, unmet expectations, and personal offences, must be investigated and resolved with humility, patience, and discernment.

Believers are called to seek transformation via the power of the Holy Spirit to regulate their anger biblically. Individuals can overcome unrighteous wrath and respond to God's will by growing the fruit of the Spirit—love, joy, peace, patience, kindness, goodness, faithfulness, gentleness, and self-control.

Finally, the biblical notion of anger includes both righteous and unjustified emotions. It emphasises the significance of distinguishing between the two and responding properly. Understanding the causes and effects of anger and the invitation to practise self-control and seek transformation by the Holy Spirit enables people to manage their anger to reflect God's character and promote holiness.

Questions for Reflection

How do I personally define and understand anger, considering the biblical perspective?

Am I aligning my understanding of anger with the principles and teachings found in the Bible?

How am I currently managing and expressing my anger?

Are my responses to anger in line with the biblical principles of self-control, forgiveness, and love, or do I need to adjust to better reflect God's view of anger?

2.3 Examples of Anger in the Bible

Examples of anger in the Bible provide valuable insights into the complexities of human emotions and offer lessons on how to manage and respond to anger. Throughout Scripture, we find numerous instances where characters, including God, Jesus, and individuals, express anger in various circumstances. In this discussion, we will explore several prominent examples of anger in the Bible, examining the context, motivations, and outcomes of these instances.

One significant example of anger in the Bible is the righteous anger displayed by Jesus towards the religious leaders in the Temple. In Matthew 21:12-13, Jesus entered the Temple area and found merchants and moneychangers exploiting the sacred space for their gain. Filled with righteous indignation, Jesus overturned the tables and drove out those who were buying and selling, exclaiming, "It is written, 'My house will be called a house of prayer,' but you are making it a den of robbers'" (Matthew 21:13).

This example of Jesus' anger highlights his zeal for God's house's holiness and proper reverence. It serves as a reminder that there are times when anger can be justified in the face of corruption, exploitation, and the dishonouring of sacred things. Jesus' display of anger demonstrates the importance of upholding God's standards and defending righteousness.

Another example of anger in the Bible is found in the life of Moses. In Exodus 32:19-20, after Moses came down from Mount Sinai with the tablets containing the Ten Commandments, he witnessed the Israelites worshipping a golden calf they had made. Outraged by their idolatry and disobedience, Moses threw the tablets to the ground, breaking them in anger.

Moses' anger was motivated by his deep concern for the people's relationship with God and their covenant violation. This example highlights the tension between God's righteous standards and humanity's rebelliousness. While Moses' anger was justifiable, his response also serves as a cautionary tale, illustrating the importance of managing anger in a way that aligns with God's purposes.

In addition to Jesus and Moses, there are instances in the Bible where God expresses anger. In Numbers 25:3-4, God's anger was kindled against the Israelites when they engaged in sexual immorality and idolatry with the Moabite women. This anger resulted in a devastating plague that afflicted the people.

These examples of God's anger emphasise the significance of upholding His commands and the consequences that can arise from disobedience. However, they also demonstrate God's desire for repentance and restoration. In Exodus 32:11-14, Moses interceded on behalf of the Israelites, appealing to God's mercy and compassion, leading to avert God's wrath and punishment. These instances of anger from God teach us about the seriousness of sin and the need for repentance and seeking His forgiveness.

Apart from these significant examples, the Bible also contains instances of human anger that serve as cautionary tales. In the story of Cain and Abel (Genesis 4:5-8), Cain's anger towards his brother Abel due to jealousy and the rejection of his offering led him to commit the first murder. This account highlights the destructive consequences of uncontrolled anger and the importance of addressing negative emotions before they lead to sinful actions.

Similarly, in the story of King Saul's anger towards David (1 Samuel 18:7-9), Saul's jealousy and rage consumed him, leading to a prolonged pursuit of David's life. Saul's unrighteous anger damaged his relationship with David. It resulted in the loss of his kingdom and the withdrawal of God's favour.

These examples of anger in the Bible reveal this powerful emotion's complexities and potential dangers. They demonstrate that while anger can sometimes be justified or understandable, it is crucial to exercise self-control, seek God's guidance, and respond in ways that align with His character and purposes.

The examples of anger in the Bible also teach the importance of addressing and resolving anger promptly and constructively. In Ephesians 4:26-27, the apostle Paul instructs believers, "In your anger, do not sin: Do not let the sun go down while you are still angry, and do not give the devil a foothold." This verse highlights the need to address anger promptly, seeking reconciliation, forgiveness, and resolution.

The Bible encourages believers to cultivate virtues that counteract anger. Galatians 5:22-23 describes the fruit of the Spirit, which includes love, joy, peace, patience, kindness, goodness, faithfulness, gentleness, and self-control. These qualities, nurtured through the Holy Spirit's work, help believers manage their anger and respond in ways that reflect God's character.

It is important to note that the examples of anger in the Bible do not provide a blanket endorsement of anger as a valid response in every situation. Rather, they illustrate how anger can be expressed righteously or unrighteously and highlight the need for discernment, self-reflection, and seeking God's guidance in managing our emotions.

The Bible presents various examples of anger, including the righteous anger of Jesus and Moses and instances of God's anger towards disobedience and idolatry. These examples teach the importance of upholding God's standards, addressing sin, and seeking restoration. They also caution against uncontrolled anger, which can lead to destructive consequences. By studying these examples and applying biblical principles, believers can gain insight into managing their anger, resolving conflicts, and responding in ways that reflect God's love, mercy, and righteousness.

Questions for Reflection

As I consider the examples of anger in the Bible, how do they challenge or resonate with my own experiences of anger?

What can I learn from these biblical examples regarding managing and responding to my anger righteously and constructively?

Are any patterns or triggers consistently leading to uncontrolled or unrighteous anger in my life?

How can I seek God's guidance and apply biblical principles to address and transform these areas of struggle?

2.4 God's View on Anger

Understanding God's view of anger is crucial for developing a biblical perspective on this powerful emotion. The Bible provides insights into how God perceives and responds to anger, shedding light on His character, His desires for His people, and the righteous standards He upholds. In this discussion, we will explore God's view of anger, examining His nature, His expressions, and His teachings on how humans should manage anger.

First and foremost, it is important to acknowledge that God's anger is distinct from human anger. God's anger is rooted in His holiness, righteousness, and perfect justice. Unlike human anger, which can often be tainted by selfishness, pride, and a desire for revenge, God's anger is pure and directed towards what is contrary to His nature and will. Psalm 7:11 affirms, "God is a righteous judge, a God who displays his wrath daily."

The Bible presents instances where God expresses anger towards human sin and rebellion. In Exodus 32:9-10, for example, God's anger burned against the Israelites when they worshipped the golden calf they had made while Moses was on Mount Sinai. God's anger in this context arose from the people's blatant idolatry and violation of the covenant. His righteous anger is a testament to His holiness and the seriousness of sin.

However, it is important to note that God's anger is never capricious or impulsive. His anger is always just and measured. Exodus 34:6-7 describes God as "slow to anger and abounding in love and faithfulness." This passage demonstrates God's patience, mercy, and desire to extend forgiveness and offer opportunities for repentance.

God's anger is often accompanied by a call to repentance and a desire for reconciliation. In the Old Testament, prophets like Jeremiah and Ezekiel frequently conveyed God's anger against the unfaithfulness of His people. Yet, even in His anger, God longed for His people to turn from their wicked ways and return to Him. Ezekiel 18:30-32 conveys this sentiment: "Repent! Turn away from all your offences; then sin will not be your downfall... For I take no pleasure in the death of anyone, declares the Sovereign LORD. Repent and live!"

God's view of anger is also reflected in His teachings and instructions to His people. In several passages, the Bible advises believers to exercise self-control and manage their anger in a way consistent with God's character. Proverbs 14:29 states, "Whoever is patient has great understanding, but one who is quick-tempered displays folly." This verse highlights the value of patience and self-control, underscoring the importance of managing anger wisely and righteously.

The New Testament provides additional guidance on how believers should respond to anger. In Ephesians 4:26-27, Paul writes, "In your anger, do not sin: Do not let the sun go down while you are still angry, and do not give the devil a foothold." This passage emphasises the need to address and resolve anger promptly, guarding against sin and the potentially destructive consequences of unresolved anger.

Jesus' teachings in the Sermon on the Mount provide profound insights into God's view of anger. In Matthew 5:21-22, Jesus states, "You have heard that it was said to the people long ago, 'You shall not murder, and anyone who murders will be subject to judgment.' But I tell you that anyone angry with a brother or sister will be subject to judgment." This teaching highlights the seriousness of anger and its potential to lead to sinful actions and broken relationships.

However, it is important to note that God's view of anger is not solely focused on condemnation and judgment. While He despises sin and rebellion, He also offers forgiveness, reconciliation, and transformation. God's ultimate desire is for His people to experience healing and restoration.

In the New Testament, we see the embodiment of God's character and His perspective on anger through Jesus Christ. Jesus, being fully

God and fully human, provides the perfect example of righteous anger and self-control. In Mark 3:5, Jesus looks at the Pharisees with anger and grief because of their hardness of heart. Yet, He responds with compassion and performs acts of healing on the Sabbath, demonstrating love and mercy even in His anger.

God's view of anger is intertwined with His love and grace. In Romans 5:8, the apostle Paul writes, "But God demonstrates his love for us in this: While we were still sinners, Christ died for us." This verse reminds us that even in the face of human sin and rebellion that deserved God's anger, He chose to extend His love and offer a path to salvation through Jesus Christ. God's anger is balanced by His unfailing love and desire to reconcile humanity to Himself.

Ultimately, God's view of anger calls us to examine our hearts and attitudes. He calls us to manage our anger in a way that reflects His character and aligns with His purposes. James 1:19-20 provides valuable guidance: "My dear brothers and sisters, take note of this: Everyone should be quick to listen, slow to speak and slow to become angry because human anger does not produce the righteousness that God desires."

God's view of anger is multifaceted and rooted in His holiness, righteousness, and perfect justice. While God's anger is expressed against sin and rebellion, it is always measured, just, and accompanied by a call to repentance and reconciliation. God's view of anger also emphasises the importance of self-control, patience, and wisdom in managing our anger. Ultimately, God's view of anger is characterised by His love, grace, and desire for humanity's redemption. By seeking His guidance, we can navigate our anger in a way that reflects His character and brings glory to His name.

Questions for Reflection

How does my understanding of God's view of anger impact how I perceive and handle my anger?

Am I aligning my perspective on anger with God's character and teachings as revealed in Scripture?

How can I grow in embodying God's perspective on anger, including expressing righteous anger when appropriate, seeking reconciliation and forgiveness, and managing my anger to reflect His love, mercy, and grace?

3. The Consequences of Uncontrolled Anger

When left unchecked and uncontrolled, anger can have severe consequences. It can wreak havoc on our well-being, relationships, and overall quality of life. The consequences of uncontrolled anger are far-reaching and can impact us and those around us.

This chapter will explore the profound consequences of uncontrolled anger and its detrimental effects on various aspects of our lives. We will examine anger's physical, emotional, and mental toll on our well-being. We will explore its destructive impact on our relationships with God and others. Through the lens of Scripture, we will gain insights into the consequences of anger and discover the pathway to healing and restoration.

The Bible provides wisdom, warnings, and examples that reveal the destructive nature of anger and its consequences. From the narratives of individuals who succumbed to anger's grip and faced dire repercussions to the teachings of Jesus and the apostles on the importance of managing anger, we are guided to understand the weightiness of this emotion.

As we explore the consequences of uncontrolled anger, it is essential to approach this topic with humility and a sincere desire for growth. Acknowledging our struggles with anger and the potential harm it can cause is the first step towards transformation. We must be willing to confront our shortcomings, seek forgiveness, and take steps towards healing and restoration.

Throughout this chapter, we will explore practical strategies and biblical principles that can help us overcome uncontrolled anger and its consequences. We will reflect on the importance of self-awareness, emotional regulation, and seeking God's guidance in managing our anger. By aligning our hearts and actions with the teachings of

Scripture, we can experience the freedom and peace that come from releasing the destructive grip of anger.

May this chapter serve as a guide and source of encouragement as we navigate the challenges of anger and its consequences. Together, let us embark on a journey of self-reflection, growth, and transformation as we strive to honour God in our thoughts, words, and actions.

"But now you must also rid yourselves of all such things as these: anger, rage, malice, slander, and filthy language from your lips" (Colossians 3:8, NIV).

Prayer

Gracious and loving Father,

We come before You in humility and gratitude, recognising Your sovereignty and the power of Your Word to transform our lives. As we reflect on the contents of this chapter, we acknowledge the sobering reality of the consequences of uncontrolled anger.

Lord, we confess that anger can easily consume us, leading us down a destructive path. We have witnessed its damaging effects on our relationships and well-being and witness it as Your children. Today, we humbly seek Your forgiveness for the times we have allowed anger to gain control over our hearts and actions.

In this chapter, we have explored the far-reaching consequences of uncontrolled anger. We have learned how it can damage relationships, erode trust, and hinder spiritual growth. As we reflect on these truths, we ask for Your guidance and strength to address and surrender our anger to You.

Father, we pray that Your Spirit will illuminate areas of our lives where anger has taken root. Give us the courage to confront our anger, to acknowledge its destructive impact, and to take responsibility for our actions. Help us to cultivate a spirit of self-control and restraint, knowing that it is only through Your grace and strength that we can overcome the temptations of anger.

As we consider the consequences of uncontrolled anger, we also reflect on the example of Jesus Christ. He faced provocations and injustices but responded with love, compassion, and grace. Lord, we pray that You would mould us into His likeness, that we may be vessels of Your peace and agents of reconciliation in a world filled with anger.

Grant us the wisdom to seek reconciliation where there is brokenness and to extend forgiveness to those who have wronged us. Help us to be mindful of our words and actions so that they may reflect

Your love and grace to others. May we be instruments of healing and restoration, guided by the principles of Your Word.

Father, we acknowledge that overcoming uncontrolled anger requires surrendering to Your will. Fill us with Your Holy Spirit to transform us from within. Give us the strength to resist the temptations of anger and to respond with patience, kindness, and gentleness.

We pray for Your divine wisdom to guide us in all our interactions. Teach us to communicate effectively, with humility and empathy, seeking understanding rather than seeking to win arguments. May our words be seasoned with grace and build others up rather than tearing them down.

Thank You, Lord, for our lessons in this chapter. We surrender our anger to You, trusting in Your power to bring healing and restoration. Help us to walk in the freedom that comes from surrendering our anger to Your loving and compassionate care.

In Jesus' name, we pray.

Amen.

3.1 Destructive Effects on personal well-being

Anger, when left unchecked and unmanaged, can have severe negative impacts on an individual's personal well-being. It affects a person's emotional and mental state and can have physical and relational consequences. In this discussion, we will explore the destructive effects of uncontrolled anger on personal well-being, examining its toll on mental health, physical health, and relationships.

Mental Health Implications: Uncontrolled anger can significantly impact a person's mental health, leading to various negative consequences. One of the primary mental health issues associated with unmanaged anger is increased stress levels. Proverbs 14:17 states, "A quick-tempered person does foolish things, and the one who devises evil schemes is hated." Persistent anger and stress activate the body's fight-or-flight response, continuously releasing stress hormones like cortisol. Prolonged exposure to high levels of cortisol can contribute to anxiety, depression, and other mental health disorders.

Uncontrolled anger can lead to the development or exacerbation of anger-related disorders, such as intermittent explosive disorder (IED). IED is characterised by recurrent, explosive outbursts of anger disproportionate to the situation. Proverbs 29:22 warns, "An angry person stirs up conflict, and a hot-tempered person commits many sins." These outbursts can cause significant distress and impair an individual's ability to function effectively in their daily life.

Unmanaged anger can fuel a negative cycle of rumination and bitterness. When individuals hold onto anger and resentment, they often replay the perceived offences in their minds, leading to a heightened state of anger and distress. Proverbs 15:18 advises, "A hot-tempered person stirs up conflict, but the one who is patient calms a quarrel." This continuous rumination can lead to increased bitterness, reduced self-esteem, and a negative worldview.

Physical Health Consequences: Uncontrolled anger not only affects mental health but also has detrimental effects on physical well-being. Research has shown that chronic anger and hostility are associated with various physical health problems, including cardiovascular issues, high blood pressure, and compromised immune function.

Proverbs 14:30 states, "A heart at peace gives life to the body, but envy rots the bones." This verse highlights the connection between inner peace and physical health. The constant activation of the body's stress response due to unmanaged anger can contribute to chronic inflammation, which has been linked to a range of health conditions, including heart disease, diabetes, and autoimmune disorders.

Uncontrolled anger can manifest in aggressive behaviour, potentially leading to physical harm to oneself or others. Proverbs 29:11 warns, "Fools give full vent to their rage, but the wise bring calm in the end." Acts of aggression and violence resulting from unmanaged anger not only cause immediate physical harm but can also have long-term legal and social consequences, further deteriorating personal well-being.

Relationship Strain: Uncontrolled anger can place a significant strain on relationships, leading to damaged connections, broken trust, and isolation. Proverbs 22:24 advises, "Do not make friends with a hot-tempered person; do not associate with one easily angered." When individuals consistently display uncontrolled anger, it can become challenging for others to feel safe, respected, and valued in their presence.

Unmanaged anger often leads to communication breakdowns, escalating conflicts, and emotional distance. The destructive words spoken in the heat of anger can inflict deep wounds on loved ones and hinder the process of forgiveness and reconciliation. Proverbs 15:1

reminds us, "A gentle answer turns away wrath, but a harsh word stirs up anger." Responding to others in anger with harsh words and aggression only perpetuates a cycle of hostility and damage within relationships.

Uncontrolled anger can lead to social isolation and a loss of support systems. People may distance themselves from individuals who consistently display anger issues, fearing the unpredictable and volatile nature of such interactions. This isolation further compounds feelings of anger, frustration, and loneliness, negatively impacting personal well-being.

The negative effects of unmanaged anger can extend beyond immediate relationships to professional settings. Anger outbursts and a lack of emotional control can lead to strained relationships with colleagues, superiors, or subordinates. It can hinder teamwork, productivity, and career advancement. Proverbs 14:29 cautions, "Whoever is patient has great understanding, but one who is quick-tempered displays folly." Demonstrating patience and emotional control in the workplace is essential for maintaining positive working relationships and achieving personal success.

To mitigate the destructive effects of anger on personal well-being, it is crucial to develop effective anger management strategies rooted in biblical principles. This includes cultivating self-awareness, practising self-control, and seeking guidance from God's Word. Proverbs 16:32 encourages, "Better a patient person than a warrior, one with self-control than one who takes a city." Developing the fruit of the Spirit, such as self-control, love, and patience (Galatians 5:22-23), can aid in managing anger constructively and nurturing healthier relationships.

Seeking professional help, such as counselling or therapy, can provide valuable support in addressing deep-rooted anger issues. Therapy can help individuals explore the underlying causes of their anger, develop healthier coping mechanisms, and learn effective communication and conflict-resolution skills.

Uncontrolled anger can have significant destructive effects on personal well-being. It impacts mental health, leading to increased stress, anxiety, and anger-related disorders. It also compromises physical health, contributing to cardiovascular problems and weakened immune function. Unmanaged anger strains relationships, leading to broken trust, isolation, and damaged connections. However, by embracing biblical principles, developing self-control, and seeking help, individuals can break free from the destructive cycle of anger, experience personal growth, and foster healthier relationships. Proverbs 19:11 reminds us, "A person's wisdom yields patience; it is to one's glory to overlook an offence." With God's guidance and the willingness to change, we can find healing, restoration, and a greater sense of well-being in managing our anger according to His principles.

Questions for Reflection

How has uncontrolled anger impacted my personal well-being in terms of my mental health, physical health, and relationships?

What areas have been negatively affected, and how can I improve my well-being?

How can I develop healthier strategies for managing and expressing anger to mitigate its destructive effects on my well-being?

How can I incorporate biblical principles of self-control, forgiveness, and love into my approach to anger management?

3.2 Impact on Relationships

Uncontrolled anger has significant destructive effects on relationships. It can damage trust, communication, and intimacy, leading to strained connections, broken bonds, and emotional distress. In this discussion, we will explore the impact of uncontrolled anger on relationships, highlighting its detrimental effects and the importance of managing anger healthily and biblically.

Trust and Emotional Safety: Uncontrolled anger erodes trust within relationships. When expressed in a volatile and aggressive manner, anger creates an atmosphere of fear, uncertainty, and emotional instability. Proverbs 22:24 warns, "Do not make friends with a hot-tempered person; do not associate with one easily angered." A pattern of explosive anger can make it difficult for others to feel safe, valued, and understood.

Repeated episodes of uncontrolled anger can lead to broken promises, hurtful words, and emotional wounds that can take a long time to heal. Proverbs 11:29 states, "Whoever brings ruin on their family will inherit only wind, and the fool will be a servant to the wise." When anger damages the foundation of trust, rebuilding and restoring healthy relationships becomes challenging.

Communication Breakdown: Unmanaged anger often leads to communication breakdowns within relationships. When anger is expressed through aggressive or hurtful language, it hinders effective communication and understanding. Proverbs 15:1 advises, "A gentle answer turns away wrath, but a harsh word stirs up anger." Harsh words spoken in the heat of anger can escalate conflicts, cause emotional harm, and create a barrier to resolving issues.

Uncontrolled anger can prevent individuals from actively listening to others. When consumed by anger, individuals may be more focused on expressing their own frustrations rather than empathising and understanding the perspectives of others. Proverbs 18:13 emphasises the importance of listening, stating, "To answer before listening—that is folly and shame." Failing to listen and consider the feelings and concerns of others can lead to further misunderstandings and deepening relationship rifts.

Emotional Distress and Resentment: Unmanaged anger often leads to emotional distress and resentment within relationships. When anger is not addressed and resolved healthily, it can breed bitterness, grudges, and a desire for revenge. Proverbs 19:11 reminds us, "A person's wisdom yields patience; it is to one's glory to overlook an offence." Cultivating patience and choosing to overlook offences can prevent the accumulation of anger and resentment.

Uncontrolled anger can create a toxic cycle of negative emotions, where one person's anger triggers the anger of others, leading to a back-and-forth exchange of hurtful words and actions. Proverbs 15:18 cautions, "A hot-tempered person stirs up conflict, but the one who is patient calms a quarrel." Responding with patience, understanding, and forgiveness can help break this destructive cycle and foster healthier, more peaceful interactions.

Impact on Children and Family Dynamics: Uncontrolled anger within family dynamics can have a profound and lasting impact on children and the overall well-being of the family unit. When anger becomes a prevalent feature of family life, it creates an unstable and hostile environment that affects children's emotional development, sense of security, and self-esteem. Ephesians 6:4 instructs parents, "Fathers, do not provoke your children to anger, but bring them up in the discipline and instruction of the Lord." It emphasises the importance of nurturing an atmosphere of love, patience, and understanding within the family.

Uncontrolled anger can also strain marital relationships, leading to marital discord and potential breakdown. Frequent anger outbursts, unresolved conflicts, and a lack of emotional intimacy can gradually erode the bond between spouses. Proverbs 14:29 advises, "Whoever is patient has great understanding, but one who is quick-tempered displays folly." Patience and understanding are essential for nurturing a healthy and harmonious marital relationship.

To mitigate the destructive effects of uncontrolled anger on relationships, it is crucial to develop healthy anger management strategies rooted in biblical principles. This includes cultivating self-control, practising forgiveness, and seeking reconciliation. Ephesians 4:26-27 teaches, "In your anger do not sin: Do not let the sun go down while you are still angry, and do not give the devil a foothold." It highlights the importance of addressing and resolving anger before it festers and causes further damage.

Effective communication is also vital in managing anger and maintaining healthy relationships. Proverbs 15:1 encourages a gentle response to diffuse anger and promote understanding. By actively listening, expressing oneself calmly and respectfully, and seeking to understand the perspectives of others, conflicts can be resolved more constructively.

Embracing the biblical principles of love and forgiveness is essential in overcoming the negative effects of anger on relationships. Colossians 3:13 reminds us, "Bear with each other and forgive one another if you have a grievance against someone. Forgive as the Lord forgave you." Choosing to forgive and extend grace to others, even in anger, can foster healing, restore trust, and promote reconciliation.

When seeking to manage anger and its impact on relationships, seeking help and support is essential. This may include seeking counselling, therapy, or guidance from trusted mentors or spiritual leaders. Proverbs 12:15 advises, "The way of fools seems right to them, but the wise listen to advice." Seeking guidance from wise and experienced individuals can provide valuable insights and tools for managing anger and fostering healthier relationships.

Uncontrolled anger has significant destructive effects on relationships. It undermines trust, hampers communication, and breeds emotional distress and resentment. However, by embracing biblical principles of self-control, forgiveness, and love, individuals can break free from the destructive cycle of anger and nurture healthier and more fulfilling relationships. Through patience, understanding, effective communication, and a willingness to seek help when needed, individuals can experience healing, restoration, and the restoration of healthy and harmonious relationships. May we strive to manage our anger in a manner that honours God and uplifts those around us, cultivating relationships that reflect His love and grace.

Questions for Reflection

How has uncontrolled anger affected my relationships with others?

Have I noticed any patterns of communication breakdown, trust issues, or emotional distress resulting from my anger?

How can I develop healthier strategies for managing anger and fostering positive relationships?

How can I apply biblical principles of self-control, forgiveness, and effective communication to improve my interactions with others?

3.3 Spiritual implications

Uncontrolled anger not only has destructive effects on personal well-being and relationships but also carries significant spiritual implications. When mismanaged and allowed to consume our hearts, anger can hinder our spiritual growth, damage our relationship with God, and hinder our ability to reflect His love and grace. In this discussion, we will explore the spiritual implications of uncontrolled anger, highlighting its detrimental effects and the importance of managing anger in a way that aligns with biblical principles.

Strained Relationship with God: Uncontrolled anger can strain our relationship with God. When anger becomes a dominant force in our lives, it can overshadow our connection with the Lord and hinder our ability to experience His presence and guidance. Psalm 37:8 advises, "Refrain from anger and turn from wrath; do not fret—it leads only to evil." Allowing anger to fester and dominate our hearts hinders our ability to fully surrender to God's will and seek His guidance.

Uncontrolled anger can lead to resentment and bitterness towards God. When we become angry at the circumstances of our lives or feel a sense of injustice, it is easy to question God's goodness and sovereignty. Jonah 4:4 reveals Jonah's anger towards God when he says, "I knew that you are a gracious and compassionate God, slow to anger and abounding in love, a God who relents from sending calamity." Jonah's anger stemmed from his perception of God's mercy towards Nineveh. In such moments, we must be cautious not to allow anger to distort our view of God's character and His plans for us.

Hindrance to Spiritual Growth: Uncontrolled anger hinders our spiritual growth and maturity. When anger takes control, it can prevent us from fully embracing the fruits of the Spirit, such as love, joy, peace, patience, kindness, goodness, faithfulness, gentleness, and self-control (Galatians 5:22-23). James 1:19-20 reminds us, "My dear brothers and sisters, take note of this: Everyone should be quick to listen, slow to speak and to become angry because human anger does not produce the righteousness that God desires." Pursuing righteousness requires self-control over our anger and responding with love and grace.

Uncontrolled anger also hinders our ability to forgive and extend grace to others. Ephesians 4:31-32 teaches, "Get rid of all bitterness, rage and anger, brawling and slander, along with every malice. Be kind and compassionate to one another, forgiving each other, just as in Christ God forgave you." Holding onto anger and refusing to forgive others goes against God's command to love and forgive as He has loved and forgiven us.

Distorted Reflection of God's Character: Uncontrolled anger distorts our ability to reflect God's character to the world. As believers, we are called to be ambassadors of Christ, displaying His love, mercy, and grace in our interactions with others. Ephesians 4:26-27 warns, "In your anger do not sin: Do not let the sun go down while you are still angry, and do not give the devil a foothold." Allowing anger to control us opens the door for the enemy to manipulate our emotions and actions, tarnishing our witness as followers of Christ.

Our response to anger should reflect God's nature. James 1:20 reminds us, "Human anger does not produce the righteousness God desires." Instead, we are called to respond with grace and love, even in the face of provocation. Romans 12:21 encourages us, "Do not be overcome by evil, but overcome evil by good." By overcoming anger with good, we reflect the transformative power of God's love and demonstrate His character to those around us.

Need for Repentance and Restoration: Uncontrolled anger requires repentance and a commitment to seek restoration with God and others. When our anger causes harm or strife, we must humble ourselves, seek forgiveness, and make amends. Matthew 5:23-24 instructs, "Therefore, if you are offering your gift at the altar and there remember that your brother or sister has something against you, leave your gift there in front of the altar. First, go and be reconciled to them;

then come and offer your gift." This verse emphasises the significance of resolving conflicts and seeking reconciliation as a priority in our relationship with God.

Repentance involves acknowledging our sinful response to anger, seeking forgiveness from God, and allowing His transformative power to work in our hearts. It requires a commitment to change, relying on the Holy Spirit's guidance to cultivate a spirit of love, gentleness, and self-control.

Seeking restoration also means actively pursuing healing and reconciliation in damaged relationships. This involves engaging in open and honest communication, listening to the concerns of others, and extending forgiveness and grace. Colossians 3:13 encourages, "Bear with each other and forgive one another if any of you has a grievance against someone. Forgive as the Lord forgave you." Through the power of forgiveness, we demonstrate God's love and grace, fostering reconciliation and restoration.

Uncontrolled anger has significant spiritual implications. It strains our relationship with God, hinders our spiritual growth, distorts our reflection of God's character, and calls for repentance and restoration. Biblically managing anger requires surrendering our emotions to God, cultivating the fruits of the Spirit, seeking forgiveness, extending grace, and actively pursuing reconciliation. By aligning our anger with God's principles, we can experience spiritual growth, reflect on His character, and deepen our connection. May we continually seek His guidance and rely on His transformative power to manage our anger in a way that honours Him and fosters spiritual well-being.

Questions for Reflection

How does my uncontrolled anger impact my spiritual journey and relationship with God?

Am I aware of any hindrances or barriers it creates in my ability to grow spiritually and reflect God's character?

How can I align my anger management with biblical principles and seek repentance and restoration in areas where my anger has caused harm or strained relationships?

How can I actively cultivate the fruits of the Spirit in my response to anger and reflect God's love and grace to those around me?

4. Seeking God's Guidance in Anger Management

Anger is an emotion that every human being experiences. It can arise from various sources, such as frustration, injustice, or personal offence. While anger is not inherently sinful, handling and managing it is very important. Uncontrolled anger can lead to destructive behaviours, damaged relationships, and a compromised witness for Christ.

This chapter will explore the significance of seeking God's guidance in anger management. Recognising that God is the ultimate source of wisdom and transformation, we turn to His Word to understand His perspective on anger and learn how to effectively manage this powerful emotion in a way that honours Him.

The Bible serves as our ultimate guide in navigating the complexities of anger. It provides timeless truths, practical wisdom, and examples of individuals who triumphed or stumbled in their anger handling. By studying and applying the principles found in Scripture, we can gain insights into God's heart for anger management and discover the path to living a life that reflects His grace and righteousness.

This chapter will explore biblical passages that address anger and its management. We will explore key teachings from the Old and New Testaments, including the words of Jesus Christ, who provides profound insights into transforming our hearts and minds. By internalising and applying these biblical principles, we can experience personal growth, develop healthier relationships, and become effective ambassadors of God's love and truth.

We will explore practical strategies for seeking God's guidance in the heat of the moment when anger arises. Through prayer, a meditation on Scripture, and reliance on the Holy Spirit, we can cultivate a heart that is receptive to God's leading, enabling us to respond to anger with grace, wisdom, and self-control.

It is important to approach the topic of anger management with humility and a willingness to examine our own hearts and attitudes. We all have growth areas, and recognising our need for God's guidance is crucial in our journey towards anger management. As we explore this chapter, let us come with open hearts and minds, ready to learn from God's Word and apply His principles to our lives.

May this chapter be a source of encouragement and practical guidance as we seek to manage our anger in a way that pleases God and brings transformation to ourselves and those around us. Let us invite God to be the central authority in our anger management, trusting Him to work in and through us as we surrender to His will.

"Be angry and do not sin; do not let the sun go down on your anger and give no opportunity to the devil" (Ephesians 4:26-27, ESV).

Prayer

Heavenly Father,

We come before You with humble hearts, seeking Your guidance and wisdom in anger management. We acknowledge that anger is a powerful emotion that can easily lead us astray without Your wisdom and grace.

Lord, we have explored the importance of seeking Your guidance in managing our anger in this chapter. We have learned that You are our ultimate source of wisdom and understanding. We can find the strength and tools to overcome anger by seeking You in prayer and studying Your Word.

Father, we confess that there have been times when our anger has gotten the best of us. We have allowed it to control our words and actions, hurting those around us and damaging our relationships. We ask for Your forgiveness for our lack of self-control and for not seeking Your guidance in those moments of anger.

As we reflect on the contents of this chapter, we are reminded of Your love and grace towards us. You are a patient and compassionate God, slow to anger and abounding in love. Help us to imitate Your character and to respond to anger with grace and humility.

Lord, we pray for the strength to surrender our anger to You. Help us to let go of bitterness, resentment, and the desire for revenge. Teach us to forgive as You have forgiven us, knowing that true healing and reconciliation can only come through Your grace.

In our journey to manage anger, we ask Your Holy Spirit to guide us. Give us discernment to recognise the triggers and patterns that lead to anger. Grant us the wisdom to pause and seek Your perspective before reacting angrily. Fill our hearts with Your love and peace so that we may respond to difficult situations with patience, understanding, and self-control.

Father, we acknowledge that seeking Your guidance in anger management is a lifelong process. We cannot do it on our own strength but only through Your power working in us. Help us continually rely on You and seek Your presence and counsel in moments of frustration and anger.

As we apply the principles of seeking Your guidance in anger management, may our lives testify to Your transformative power. May we become vessels of Your peace and love, reflecting Your character to a world needing healing and reconciliation.

Thank You, Father, for Your faithfulness and grace. We trust in Your guidance and commit ourselves to walk in the path of righteousness, seeking Your will in all things, including managing our anger.

In Jesus' name, we pray.

Amen.

4.1 Prayer and Seeking Divine Wisdom

In the anger management journey, prayer and seeking divine wisdom are vital in helping individuals navigate their emotions, gain insight, and cultivate healthy responses. Through prayer, we establish a direct line of communication with God, expressing our concerns, seeking His guidance, and inviting His transformative power into our lives. By seeking divine wisdom, we tap into God's limitless understanding and discernment, enabling us to navigate challenging situations with clarity and grace. This discussion will explore the significance of prayer and seeking divine wisdom in anger management, highlighting the biblical foundation and practical implications.

The Power of Prayer: Prayer is a powerful tool for managing anger, allowing us to bring our emotions, struggles, and desires before God. Philippians 4:6-7 encourages believers, saying, "Do not be anxious about anything, but in every situation, by prayer and petition, with thanksgiving, present your requests to God. And the peace of God, which transcends all understanding, will guard your hearts and minds in Christ Jesus." Prayer provides an avenue to release our burdens, seek guidance, and experience the peace that comes from entrusting our anger to God.

Prayer also invites God's intervention in transforming our hearts and aligning them with His will. Psalm 51:10 implores, "Create in me a pure heart, O God, and renew a steadfast spirit within me." As we seek God's presence and surrender our anger to Him, He can purify our hearts, replace our destructive emotions with His love and compassion, and equip us with the strength to manage anger in a healthy and God-honouring way.

Seeking Divine Wisdom: Seeking divine wisdom involves humbly acknowledging our need for guidance and understanding and relying on God's Word and the Holy Spirit to navigate our emotions and responses. James 1:5 assures us, "If any of you lacks wisdom, you should ask God, who gives generously to all without finding fault, and it will be given to you." When faced with anger-inducing situations, seeking divine wisdom enables us to see beyond our immediate emotions and gain a broader perspective rooted in God's truth.

The Bible is a rich source of divine wisdom, offering guidance on managing anger and cultivating virtues such as patience, self-control, and forgiveness. Proverbs 16:32 states, "Better a patient person than a warrior, one with self-control than one who takes a city." This verse emphasises the importance of self-control in managing anger, highlighting its value in promoting peace and constructive responses.

In seeking divine wisdom, studying relevant biblical passages that address anger and its management is crucial. Ephesians 4:31-32 advises, "Get rid of all bitterness, rage and anger, brawling and slander, along with every malice. Be kind and compassionate to one another, forgiving each other, just as in Christ God forgave you." By meditating on such passages, we gain insight into God's desires for our anger management. We are empowered to align our thoughts and actions with His will.

The Practice of Prayer and Seeking Divine Wisdom: Prayer and seeking divine wisdom are not merely theoretical concepts but active practices that require consistency, sincerity, and a posture of humility. They involve creating intentional space for communion with God, where we can express our emotions, seek His guidance, and listen for His still, small voice.

One key aspect of incorporating prayer and seeking divine wisdom into anger management is inviting the Holy Spirit's transformative work into our lives. Galatians 5:22-23 reminds us of the fruits of the Spirit: "But the fruit of the Spirit is love, joy, peace, forbearance, kindness, goodness, faithfulness, gentleness and self-control. Against such things, there is no law." When we surrender our anger to God in prayer and seek His wisdom, the Holy Spirit empowers us to bear these fruits, transforming our hearts and guiding our responses.

Practical steps can be taken to cultivate a prayerful and wisdom-seeking lifestyle in anger management. These include setting aside regular prayer and reflection, engaging in biblical study and meditation, seeking counsel from wise and mature believers, and actively listening to the promptings of the Holy Spirit.

In moments of anger, we can pause, step back, and invite God into the situation through prayer. We can ask Him for guidance, wisdom, and the strength to respond in a way that reflects His character. Through prayer, we express our emotions, invite God to intervene, and shape our perspectives, thoughts, and actions.

Seeking divine wisdom involves intentionally seeking out biblical principles and teachings on anger management. By studying relevant passages, we gain insight into God's perspective and learn from the examples set by biblical characters who faced anger-inducing situations. For example, the story of Joseph in Genesis 45 demonstrates his ability to respond to his brothers, who had betrayed him, with forgiveness and reconciliation. Such narratives provide valuable lessons on how to manage anger in a manner consistent with God's will.

Seeking counsel from wise and mature believers can provide valuable guidance and perspective. Proverbs 11:14 states, "Where there is no guidance, a people fall, but in an abundance of counsellors there is safety." Seeking the advice of those who have walked through similar struggles and have demonstrated wisdom in their own lives can offer valuable insights and accountability.

Practising prayer and seeking divine wisdom in anger management leads to transformation and growth. As we invite God into our anger, He equips us with the tools to manage it effectively, promoting peace, reconciliation, and spiritual growth.

Prayer and seeking divine wisdom are powerful practices for managing anger. Through prayer, we open ourselves to God's guidance, inviting His presence and peace into our hearts. Seeking divine wisdom involves studying His Word, meditating on relevant passages, and seeking counsel from wise believers. By incorporating these practices into our lives, we can navigate anger with wisdom and grace, aligning our responses with God's desires. May we continually seek His guidance, rely on His wisdom, and experience His transformative power as we strive to manage our anger in a way that honours Him and promotes spiritual well-being.

Questions for Reflection

Am I consistently prioritising prayer in my journey of anger management?

How can I deepen my prayer life and rely on God's guidance in navigating my emotions and responses to anger?

How actively am I seeking divine wisdom in managing my anger?

How can I study God's Word, seek counsel from wise believers, and apply biblical principles to cultivate a wise and godly approach to anger?

4.2 Studying Relevant Biblical Passages

Studying relevant biblical passages is crucial in gaining insight, guidance, and practical wisdom in the anger management journey. The Bible is a rich source of divine revelation, offering timeless truths that address the complexities of human emotions and provide a roadmap for managing anger in a way that honours God and fosters healthy relationships. By exploring and meditating on these passages, we can gain a deeper understanding of God's perspective on anger, learn from the examples set by biblical characters, and apply the principles and teachings to our lives. This discussion will explore the significance of studying relevant biblical passages in anger management, highlighting the biblical foundation and practical implications.

The Authority of God's Word: Christians recognise the Bible as the authoritative Word of God, inspired by the Holy Spirit and intended to guide believers in all aspects of life. 2 Timothy 3:16-17 states, "All Scripture is God-breathed and is useful for teaching, rebuking, correcting and training in righteousness, so that the servant of God may be thoroughly equipped for every good work." This verse affirms the divine origin of Scripture and emphasises its relevance in equipping believers for godly living.

Studying relevant biblical passages on anger management allows us to tap into God's wisdom and discern His will for our lives. It provides a foundation for understanding the nature of anger, the consequences of uncontrolled anger, and the virtues and principles that promote healthy responses. By immersing ourselves in God's Word, we open ourselves to transformation and equip ourselves with the tools needed to navigate anger in a way that reflects His character.

Biblical Examples and Narratives: The Bible contains numerous examples and narratives that offer insights into anger and its management. These stories provide practical illustrations of individuals who faced anger-inducing situations, showcasing both positive and negative responses. By studying these accounts, we can learn from their experiences, draw wisdom from their successes and failures, and apply their lessons to our lives.

One notable example is the story of Moses in Exodus 2:11-15. When Moses witnessed an Egyptian mistreating a Hebrew, his anger led him to impulsively kill the Egyptian. This impulsive response had serious consequences, as Moses had to flee and face the consequences of his actions. Through this narrative, we see the destructive effects of uncontrolled anger and the importance of managing our emotions in a way that aligns with God's principles.

On the other hand, we find examples of individuals who demonstrated godly responses to anger. In the New Testament, Jesus provides a powerful model of managing anger righteously and lovingly. In Mark 11:15-17, Jesus enters the temple and witnesses the money changers and merchants exploiting the house of God. Instead of reacting impulsively, Jesus displays controlled anger, driving out the merchants and proclaiming the rightful purpose of the temple. This narrative teaches us the importance of righteous anger when directed toward injustice or dishonouring God's name.

Principles and Teachings on Anger: Throughout the Bible, some specific principles and teachings address anger and guide how to manage it in a way that honours God. These principles highlight self-control, patience, forgiveness, and love.

Ephesians 4:26-27 offers practical guidance on anger management: "In your anger do not sin: Do not let the sun go down while you are still angry, and do not give the devil a foothold." This passage acknowledges that anger is a natural emotion but emphasises the importance of not letting it lead to sin. It encourages prompt resolution of anger and warns against harbouring resentment, which can give the enemy a foothold in our lives. This passage emphasises the need for self-control and a proactive approach to resolving anger before it festers and leads to destructive behaviours.

Another important teaching on anger is in James 1:19-20: "My dear brothers and sisters, take note of this: Everyone should be quick to listen, slow to speak and slow to become angry because human anger does not produce the righteousness that God desires." This passage highlights the value of listening attentively and exercising restraint in our speech, demonstrating the importance of thoughtful and measured responses rather than impulsive reactions driven by anger. It reminds us that our anger should not lead us away from righteousness but spur us toward godly responses.

By studying and meditating on such passages, we gain practical wisdom and guidance for managing our anger. We are encouraged to cultivate virtues such as self-control, patience, forgiveness, and love, crucial in transforming our anger into constructive actions and promoting healthy relationships. Through the power of the Holy Spirit, we can embody these virtues and reflect the character of Christ in anger-inducing situations.

Practical Steps in Studying Relevant Biblical Passages:

Adopting a systematic approach that combines reflection and application is beneficial to effectively study relevant biblical passages on anger management. Here are some practical steps to consider:

1. Identify relevant passages: Identify biblical passages that directly address anger or contain principles and teachings relevant to anger management. Examples include earlier verses such as Ephesians 4:26-27 and James 1:19-20, Proverbs 29:11, Proverbs 15:1, and Colossians 3:8.

2. Read and reflect: Take time to read and reflect on the selected passages. Engage deeply to understand the context, message, and intended audience. Consider the insights biblical commentators provide or study resources to gain a deeper understanding of the passages.

3. Internalise the principles: As you reflect on the passages,

internalise the principles and teachings. Ask yourself how these principles can be applied to your life and anger management. Consider the areas where you struggle the most and how the principles can help guide your thoughts, attitudes, and actions.

4. Prayer and meditation: Engage in prayer and meditation as you study the passages. Seek God's guidance and ask Him to reveal areas of your life that need transformation. Pray for the Holy Spirit's empowerment to embody the virtues and principles highlighted in the passages.

5. Application in daily life: The goal of studying relevant biblical passages is transformation and application in our daily lives. Consider practical ways to apply the principles and teachings in your interactions with others, especially in anger-inducing situations. Seek accountability and support from fellow believers to help you consistently walk out of these principles.

Studying relevant biblical passages is essential for gaining insight and guidance in anger management. The Bible provides timeless truths, practical examples, and teachings that equip us to navigate our anger in a way that honours God and promotes healthy relationships. By immersing ourselves in God's Word, reflecting on its wisdom, and applying its principles, we can experience transformation and growth in our ability to manage anger in a godly and constructive manner. May we approach the study of relevant biblical passages with open hearts, seeking divine wisdom and guidance as we strive to reflect the character of Christ in all aspects of our lives.

Questions for Reflection

How am I currently incorporating the study of relevant biblical passages on anger management into my spiritual life?

How can I deepen my understanding and apply these teachings daily?

In what areas of my life do I struggle the most with anger?

How can I apply the principles and teachings found in relevant biblical passages to transform my responses and promote healthy relationships in those areas?

4.3 Developing a personal relationship with God

Developing a personal relationship with God is at the core of effective anger management and overall spiritual growth. This intimate connection with our Creator provides a solid foundation for understanding His perspective on anger, seeking His guidance, and experiencing His transformative power in our lives. In this discussion, we will explore the significance of developing a personal relationship with God, explore the biblical basis for this relationship, and highlight practical steps to foster a deeper connection with Him.

The Biblical Basis of a Personal Relationship with God: The Bible presents a clear invitation from God to enter a personal relationship with Him. In the Old Testament, God revealed Himself to His people and established covenants, demonstrating His desire for an intimate connection with humanity. In Jeremiah 31:33, the Lord says, "I will put my law in their minds and write it on their hearts. I will be their God, and they will be my people." This verse reflects God's intention to have a close, personal relationship with His people, marked by His presence and guidance.

In the New Testament, through the sacrifice of Jesus Christ, the opportunity for an even deeper and more intimate relationship with God became available. In John 1:12-13, it is written, "Yet to all who did receive him, to those who believed in his name, he gave the right to become children of God—children born not of natural descent, nor of human decision or a husband's will, but born of God." Through faith in Jesus, we are adopted into God's family and granted the privilege of being His children. This relationship goes beyond a mere religious affiliation; it is a personal, familial bond characterised by love, trust, and communion with our Heavenly Father.

The Significance of a Personal Relationship with God in Anger Management: Developing a personal relationship with God is foundational to effective anger management. It transforms our perspective on anger and equips us with the resources needed to respond in a manner that aligns with God's character and will.

Knowing God's Character: A personal relationship with God enables us to know Him intimately, which includes understanding His character. As we grow closer to Him, we learn He is patient, slow to anger, compassionate, and full of grace (Exodus 34:6; Psalm 103:8). This knowledge shapes our understanding of anger, guiding us to reflect His attributes in our responses. When we encounter anger-inducing situations, we can draw upon our knowledge of God's character to inform our choices and actions.

Seeking God's Guidance: In a personal relationship with God, we seek His guidance and wisdom in all areas of life, including anger management. James 1:5-6 encourages us to ask for wisdom from God, who generously gives it to those who ask in faith. When we face challenging situations that provoke anger, we can pray to Him, seeking His guidance, discernment, and strength to respond in a way that honours Him.

Experiencing Transformation: Developing a personal relationship with God opens us to His transformative power. As we surrender ourselves to Him, allowing Him to shape our hearts and minds, we can experience His work of sanctification. This transformation affects how we process and express our anger. Galatians 5:22-23 describes the fruit of the Spirit, which includes love, joy, peace, patience, kindness, goodness, faithfulness, gentleness, and self-control. These virtues counteract the destructive tendencies of uncontrolled anger and are cultivated as we grow closer to God.

Practical Steps to Develop a Personal Relationship with God: Prayer: Prayer is essential to developing a personal relationship with God. It is a means of communication and communion with our

Heavenly Father. Through prayer, we can express our thoughts, emotions, and desires to Him. Still, more importantly, we can listen and seek His guidance and presence. Jesus Himself emphasised the significance of prayer and modelled it as an integral part of His relationship with the Father. In Matthew 6:6, He says, "But when you pray, go into your room, close the door and pray to your unseen Father. Then your Father, who sees what is done secretly, will reward you." This verse encourages us to have a private, intimate space for prayer and to cultivate a regular habit of seeking God's presence through prayer.

Study of God's Word: Developing a personal relationship with God requires actively engaging with His Word, the Bible. The Scriptures are a means through which God reveals Himself, His character, His will, and His ways. As we study and meditate on His Word, we understand who God is and how He desires us to live. 2 Timothy 3:16-17 states, "All Scripture is God-breathed and is useful for teaching, rebuking, correcting and training in righteousness, so that the servant of God may be thoroughly equipped for every good work." By immersing ourselves in the Word of God, we equip ourselves with the knowledge and wisdom necessary to navigate our lives, including managing anger godly.

Cultivating Intimacy through Worship: Worship is a powerful way to cultivate intimacy in our relationship with God. It involves expressing our love, adoration, and reverence for Him. Through worship, we acknowledge His worthiness, magnify His greatness, and surrender ourselves to His lordship. Psalm 95:6-7 says, "Come, let us bow down in worship, let us kneel before the Lord, our Maker; for he is our God, and we are the people of his pasture, the flock under his care." Engaging in corporate worship with other believers and personal worship times can deepen our connection with God and foster a sense of awe and reverence for Him.

Community and Fellowship: Developing a personal relationship with God is not meant to be an isolated journey. God designed us to be in a community with other believers. Engaging in fellowship with other Christians provides mutual encouragement, accountability, and spiritual growth opportunities. Hebrews 10:24-25 encourages us to "consider how we may spur one another on toward love and good deeds, not giving up meeting together, as some are in the habit of doing, but encouraging one another." Being part of a community of believers allows us to learn from one another, share our struggles and victories, and support each other in developing a deeper relationship with God.

Walking in Obedience: Obedience is vital to developing a personal relationship with God. Through obedience, we demonstrate our love for Him and align our lives with His will. Jesus affirms this in John 14:23 when He says, "Anyone who loves me will obey my teaching. My Father will love them, and we will come to them and make our home with them." As we seek to follow God's commands and align our actions with His Word, we invite His presence and guidance into our lives. Obedience to His commands also includes applying His teachings on anger management and seeking to respond to challenging situations with grace, forgiveness, and self-control.

Developing a personal relationship with God is foundational to effective anger management and spiritual growth. Through this relationship, we gain a deeper understanding of God's character, seek His guidance, and experience His transformative power. It involves intentional practices such as prayer, studying God's Word, cultivating intimacy through worship, engaging in community and fellowship, and walking in obedience to His commands. As we develop this personal relationship with God, we open ourselves to His wisdom, guidance, and transforming work, including managing anger. May we continually seek to deepen our connection with Him, allowing His love and grace to shape our responses and interactions, and may we experience the abundant life and peace that comes from walking closely with our Heavenly Father.

Questions for Reflection

How am I actively cultivating and nurturing my personal relationship with God?

What steps can I take to deepen my intimacy with Him and seek His guidance in managing my anger?

In what ways has my personal relationship with God impacted my approach to anger management and relationships?

How can I further align my actions and responses with His character and teachings?

5. Biblical Principles for Anger Management

Anger is a powerful and complex emotion that has the potential to impact our lives and relationships in significant ways. While experiencing anger is a natural part of being human, it is crucial to approach this emotion with wisdom and self-control. This chapter will explore the Bible's invaluable guidance in managing our anger in a way that aligns with God's heart and purposes.

The Scriptures are filled with teachings and principles that can help us navigate the challenges of anger and transform it into a force for good. God, in His infinite wisdom, has provided us with a roadmap for managing our anger in ways that honour Him and promote healthy relationships with others.

In this chapter, we will explore the rich wisdom of the Bible and discover foundational principles for anger management. From the Old Testament to the New Testament, we will explore passages that address the nature of anger, its potential consequences, and the transformative power of God's grace in our lives.

Through biblical examples, we will learn from individuals who faced anger-inducing situations and how they responded positively and negatively. From the righteous anger of Jesus overturning the tables in the temple to the lessons of patience and self-control exhibited by figures like Moses and David, we will glean insights into the righteous expression of anger and the dangers of uncontrolled rage.

We will explore key biblical teachings that guide us in managing our anger constructively. These principles include understanding the root causes of anger, practising forgiveness and reconciliation, cultivating patience and self-control, seeking God's wisdom and guidance, and relying on the transforming power of the Holy Spirit.

This chapter is not meant to provide a one-size-fits-all solution to anger management but to serve as a starting point for personal reflection, study, and application of biblical principles. We can align our thoughts, attitudes, and actions with His perfect will through a deep understanding and internalisation of God's Word.

As we embark on this journey of exploring biblical principles for anger management, let us approach it with humility, openness, and a willingness to be transformed by the Holy Spirit. May the insights gained from the Scriptures empower us to manage our anger in a way that brings healing, restoration, and reconciliation in our lives and relationships.

"For the anger of man does not produce the righteousness of God" (James 1:20, ESV).

Prayer

Gracious Heavenly Father,

We bow before Your presence with humble hearts, acknowledging You are the giver of all wisdom and understanding. We thank You for the teachings and insights we have gained through studying the biblical principles for anger management in this chapter.

Lord, we recognise that anger is a natural emotion that can easily lead us astray if not channelled and controlled according to Your Word. We confess that there have been times when we have allowed anger to consume us, resulting in hurtful words and actions that have caused pain and division. We seek Your forgiveness for those moments of weakness and ask for Your transforming power to guide us in managing our anger by Your will.

Thank You, Lord, for providing us with a blueprint for managing anger through Your Word. In the Scriptures, we find numerous examples of Your instruction and guidance on handling anger in a righteous and God-honouring manner. Help us to internalise these principles and apply them in our daily lives.

Father, we ask for Your grace and strength to cultivate a heart of patience, self-control, and humility. Teach us to be slow to anger and quick to listen, to respond with love and understanding rather than with harshness or retaliation. Enable us to put away bitterness, wrath, and malice and to replace them with kindness, compassion, and forgiveness.

Lord, in times of anger, remind us of Your own character. You are a God slow to anger and abounding in steadfast love. Help us to emulate Your patience and grace as we interact with others. Give us the wisdom to see beyond the surface and to understand the underlying causes of anger so that we may respond with empathy and compassion.

We pray for discernment to recognise the triggers and patterns that lead to anger. Grant us the ability to pause and reflect before reacting impulsively. Fill our hearts with Your peace and wisdom so we may respond in ways that bring healing and restoration rather than perpetuating strife and discord.

Father, we ask for the guidance of Your Holy Spirit to transform our hearts and minds. Help us to renew our thinking and align our attitudes with Your truth. Grant us the strength to resist the temptations of anger and to seek reconciliation and forgiveness when conflicts arise. May our actions and words reflect Your love and grace, drawing others closer to You.

Lord, we surrender our anger and desires for control and vindication to Your loving hands. Help us to trust in Your sovereignty and to believe that You work all things together for our good. In moments of frustration and anger, remind us of Your presence and unfailing love so we may find solace and strength in You.

Thank You, Father, for Your faithfulness and the transformative power of Your Word. We commit ourselves to diligently studying and applying biblical principles for anger management. May we be vessels of Your peace and reconciliation in a world that desperately needs Your healing touch.

We offer this prayer in the name of Jesus Christ, our Lord and Savior.

Amen.

5.1 Self-control and the Fruit of the Spirit

Self-control is a crucial aspect of anger management and a key component of the fruit of the Spirit described in Galatians 5:22-23. In this section, we will explore the significance of self-control, its role in managing anger, and how it aligns with the broader context of the fruit of the Spirit. By examining relevant biblical passages, we will gain insights into the importance of self-control and practical steps to cultivate this godly virtue in our lives.

Understanding Self-Control: Self-control, also referred to as temperance or self-discipline, involves the ability to govern and regulate one's emotions, desires, and actions. It is the power to restrain impulses and exercise restraint to respond thoughtfully and wisely, even in challenging situations. Self-control is not about suppressing or denying emotions but channelling them consistently with godly values and principles.

The Bible places great emphasis on self-control as a virtue. In Proverbs 25:28, it is written, "Like a city whose walls are broken through is a person who lacks self-control." This metaphor highlights the vulnerability and chaos that result from a lack of self-control. The Apostle Paul also highlights the importance of self-control in his writings. In 1 Corinthians 9:25-27, he compares the Christian life to that of an athlete, stating, "Everyone who competes in the games goes into strict training. They do it to get a crown that will not last, but we do it to get one that will last forever. Therefore, I do not run like someone running aimlessly or fight like a boxer beating the air. No, I strike a blow to my body and make it my slave so that after I have preached to others, I will not be disqualified for the prize." Here, Paul emphasises the discipline and self-control required to live out the Christian faith effectively.

Self-Control and Anger Management: Self-control is particularly relevant in the context of anger management. Anger, if left uncontrolled, can lead to destructive behaviours, damaged relationships, and negative consequences. However, self-control empowers us to respond to anger in a way that aligns with God's character and principles. It allows us to exercise restraint, choose our words and actions wisely, and seek resolution rather than perpetuating conflict.

The book of Proverbs provides valuable insights into the relationship between self-control and anger. Proverbs 16:32 states, "Better a patient person than a warrior, one with self-control than one who takes a city." This verse highlights the superiority of self-control over physical strength or aggression. It emphasises that restraining one's anger displays true strength and wisdom. Proverbs 14:29 further advises, "Whoever is patient has great understanding, but one who is quick-tempered displays folly." Patience is closely connected to self-control, enabling us to temper our immediate emotional reactions and respond with wisdom and understanding.

In the New Testament, the Apostle Paul emphasises the significance of self-control in managing anger. In Ephesians 4:26-27, he writes, "In your anger do not sin: Do not let the sun go down while you are still angry, and do not give the devil a foothold." This verse acknowledges that anger is a natural emotion, but it cautions against allowing anger to lead us into sin. Paul encourages believers to exercise self-control by addressing their anger promptly and avoiding prolonged resentment, which can allow the enemy to cause division and harm.

Self-Control within the Fruit of the Spirit: The fruit of the Spirit, described in Galatians 5:22-23 encompasses a collection of godly virtues that should be evident in the lives of believers. These virtues are interconnected and mutually reinforcing, working together to manifest the character of Christ. Self-control is one of the qualities listed among the fruit of the Spirit, indicating its importance in the Christian life and its role in shaping our responses, including how we manage anger.

When we cultivate self-control as part of the fruit of the Spirit, we allow the Holy Spirit to work in us, transforming our natural inclinations and empowering us to align our actions with God's will. It is not merely a matter of personal discipline or willpower but a surrender to the work of the Spirit within us. As we yield to the Spirit's leading, He equips us to exercise self-control and respond to anger in ways that honour God and promote reconciliation.

As a fruit of the Spirit, self-control is characterised by moderation, restraint, and disciplined living. It encompasses all our lives, thoughts, words, actions, and emotions. It enables us to respond to anger with measured and controlled reactions, resisting the urge to act impulsively or destructively. Instead, we are empowered to exercise wisdom, patience, and forgiveness, seek resolution, and maintain healthy relationships.

The connection between self-control and the other fruit of the Spirit is evident. For instance, self-control works in harmony with love, enabling us to respond to anger with kindness, compassion, and understanding. It aligns with patience, enabling us to bear with others and respond in a measured and thoughtful manner. Self-control also complements gentleness, preventing us from responding with harshness or aggression. Through the cultivation of self-control, the other fruit of the Spirit finds expression in our lives, contributing to healthy relationships and effective anger management.

Self-control is a vital virtue in managing anger and nurturing a godly character. It empowers us to respond to anger in ways that align with God's principles and promote reconciliation. Developing self-control allows the Holy Spirit to work in us, shaping our thoughts, emotions, and actions. Through prayer, a study of God's Word, and reliance on the Holy Spirit, we can cultivate self-control as part of the fruit of the Spirit, enabling us to navigate anger with wisdom, grace, and love. May we continually seek the empowering work of the

Holy Spirit, inviting Him to transform us and manifest the fruit of self-control in our lives.

Questions for Reflection

In what areas of my life do I struggle with self-control, particularly when it comes to managing anger?

How can I invite the Holy Spirit to work in me and cultivate greater self-control in those areas?

How does the presence or absence of self-control impact my relationships, particularly in anger or conflict?

What steps can I take to exercise self-control and respond in ways honouring God and promote reconciliation?

5.2 Forgiveness and letting go of Resentment

Forgiveness is a transformative and essential aspect of anger management. It involves releasing feelings of resentment, bitterness, and anger towards those who have hurt or wronged us. In this section, we will explore forgiveness's significance, biblical foundation, and profound impact on our well-being and relationships. By exploring relevant passages from the Bible, we will gain insight into the power of forgiveness and practical steps to embrace this godly virtue in managing our anger.

Understanding Forgiveness: Forgiveness is a central theme in the Bible, rooted in God's character and demonstrated through His redemptive work in Christ. It involves deliberately releasing the desire for revenge, justice, or retribution and extending grace, mercy, and love towards those who have caused harm. Forgiveness is not condoning or minimising the offence but rather a response acknowledging the pain while letting go of resentment and seeking reconciliation.

The Bible presents forgiveness as a divine command and a reflection of God's nature. In Ephesians 4:32, the Apostle Paul instructs believers, "Be kind to one another, tender-hearted, forgiving one another, as God in Christ forgave you." This verse emphasises the standard of forgiveness set by God Himself. Just as He has forgiven us through the sacrifice of Christ, we are called to extend that forgiveness to others.

The Biblical Foundation of Forgiveness: The foundation of forgiveness rests in God's redemptive plan and the sacrificial work of Jesus Christ. Through His death on the cross, Jesus paid the price for our sins, offering us forgiveness and reconciliation with God. The magnitude of God's forgiveness towards us is a powerful motivation and example for us to extend forgiveness to others.

In Matthew 18:21-22, Peter asked Jesus how many times he should forgive someone who sins against him, suggesting seven times. Jesus responded, "I do not say to you seven times, but seventy-seven times." Jesus' answer illustrates the limitless nature of forgiveness. It challenges us to embody that same spirit of forgiveness in our lives. The parable of the unforgiving servant in Matthew 18:23-35 further emphasises the importance of forgiveness and the consequences of withholding it. The servant, who had been forgiven a great debt, refused to forgive a fellow servant and, as a result, faced severe consequences. This parable highlights the hypocrisy and destructive nature of harbouring unforgiveness.

The Impact of Forgiveness: Forgiveness profoundly impacts our well-being, relationships, and spiritual growth. When we choose to forgive, we release ourselves from carrying anger, bitterness, and resentment. Unforgiveness can take a toll on our physical, emotional, and spiritual health, leading to stress, anxiety, and relational strain. However, forgiveness brings freedom, healing, and restoration.

In Colossians 3:13, Paul encourages believers, "Bear with each other and forgive one another if any of you has a grievance against someone. Forgive as the Lord forgave you." This verse emphasises the connection between forgiveness and maintaining healthy relationships. Forgiving others allows us to extend grace, promote reconciliation, and foster unity within the body of Christ.

Forgiveness is intrinsically tied to our relationship with God. In Mark 11:25, Jesus teaches, "And whenever you stand praying, forgive, if you have anything against anyone, so that your Father also who is in heaven may forgive you your trespasses." This verse highlights the relational aspect of forgiveness. Our ability to receive God's forgiveness is contingent upon our willingness to forgive others. By extending forgiveness, we align ourselves with God and open the door for His forgiveness to flow into our lives.

Steps to Embrace Forgiveness: While forgiveness is a divine command and a transformative virtue, it is not always easy. It requires vulnerability, humility, and a willingness to let go of the hurt caused by others. Here are some practical steps to embrace forgiveness:

Acknowledge the pain: Recognise and acknowledge the pain and hurt caused by others. It is important to validate our emotions and process the offence's impact.

Seek God's help: Ask God in prayer and seek His guidance and strength in extending forgiveness. Ask Him to work in your heart and let you let go of resentment.

Reflect on God's forgiveness: Meditate on the depth of God's forgiveness towards you. Consider the immense sacrifice of Jesus and the forgiveness you have received. Allow this reflection to inspire and motivate you to extend forgiveness to others.

Choose to forgive: Make a conscious decision to forgive, releasing the person who has wronged you from the debt they owe you. It may be helpful to verbalise your forgiveness privately or with the person involved.

Let go of resentment: Take intentional steps to let go of resentment and bitterness. Replace negative thoughts with positive and constructive ones. Pray for healing and ask God to help you release the grip of resentment.

Seek reconciliation when possible: Forgiveness does not always guarantee reconciliation, as it requires the willingness of both parties. However, if the opportunity arises and it is safe and appropriate, seek reconciliation and restoration in the relationship.

The Role of Forgiveness in Anger Management: Forgiveness plays a crucial role in anger management by breaking the cycle of resentment and bitterness. When we hold onto anger and refuse to forgive, it intensifies our feelings of anger and perpetuates a cycle of negativity. However, choosing forgiveness interrupts the cycle and paves the way for healing, reconciliation, and restoring relationships.

The Apostle Paul encourages believers in Ephesians 4:26-27, saying, "Be angry and do not sin; do not let the sun go down on your anger, and give no opportunity to the devil." This verse emphasises the importance of dealing with anger promptly and not allowing it to fester. Practising forgiveness prevents anger from taking root and causing further damage in our lives and relationships.

Forgiveness is a powerful and transformative virtue in managing anger. It is rooted in God's character and exemplified through His forgiveness towards us. By embracing forgiveness, we experience freedom, healing, and reconciliation. It is a process that requires God's help, reflection on His forgiveness, and a deliberate choice to release resentment. As we extend forgiveness to others, we reflect the heart of God and pave the way for transformed relationships and a healthier approach to managing anger. May we continually seek God's grace and empowerment to embrace forgiveness, trusting His redemptive work in our lives.

Questions for Reflection

In what areas of my life do I struggle with holding onto resentment and unforgiveness?

How does this impact my emotional well-being and relationships?

How can I deepen my understanding of God's forgiveness towards me and allow that understanding to shape my willingness to forgive others?

5.3 Humility and meekness

Humility and meekness are often overlooked today, which tend to exalt self-promotion, assertiveness, and personal rights. However, in anger management, these qualities are essential for cultivating healthy relationships, resolving conflicts, and experiencing personal growth. This section will explore the biblical understanding of humility and meekness, their significance in managing anger, and practical steps to develop a gentle and humble spirit.

The Biblical Foundation of Humility and Meekness: The Bible emphasises humility and meekness as virtues that reflect the character of God and the example set by Jesus Christ. In Matthew 11:29, Jesus says, "Take my yoke upon you, and learn from me, for I am gentle and lowly in heart, and you will find rest for your souls." Jesus' words highlight His humility and meekness, inviting us to learn from His example.

In Philippians 2:3-5, the Apostle Paul urges believers, "Do nothing from selfish ambition or conceit, but in humility count others more significant than yourselves. Let each of you look not only to his own interests but also to the interests of others. Have this mind among yourselves, which is yours in Christ Jesus." These verses emphasise the call to humility and the mindset of selflessness that characterised Christ's life.

Understanding Humility: Humility is a posture of the heart that recognises our limitations, weaknesses, and dependence on God. It involves properly estimating ourselves, considering God's greatness, and recognising that all our abilities, talents, and achievements are His gifts.

In James 4:6, we are reminded, "But he gives more grace. Therefore, it says, 'God opposes the proud but gives grace to the humble.'" This verse reveals the connection between humility and receiving God's grace. When we approach God humbly, acknowledging our need for Him, He extends His grace to us.

Humility is not about self-deprecation or a lack of confidence but rather an accurate understanding of ourselves in relation to God. As we embrace humility, we open ourselves to God's transforming work in our lives and His empowerment to manage anger with a gentle spirit.

Embracing Meekness: Meekness is often misunderstood as weakness, but it conveys strength under control in biblical terms. The ability to restrain one's power, passions, and responses reflects gentleness, patience, and long-suffering.

In Matthew 5:5, Jesus declares, "Blessed are the meek, for they shall inherit the earth." This beatitude highlights the value and reward of meekness. It is not about exerting dominance or seeking personal gain, but rather a willingness to submit to God's will, trusting in His sovereignty and seeking His glory above our own.

Meekness is demonstrated in our relationships, especially in conflict or anger. Instead of reacting with aggression or retaliation, a meek person responds gentleness, seeking reconciliation and restoration.

The Role of Humility and Meekness in Anger Management: Humility and meekness are pivotal in managing anger effectively and fostering healthy relationships. When we approach anger with humility, we acknowledge that our feelings and perspectives are not the ultimate truth, and we are open to considering the perspectives of others. It helps us avoid an inflated sense of entitlement or the need to prove ourselves right.

In Proverbs 15:1, we read, "A soft answer turns away wrath, but a harsh word stirs up anger." This verse emphasises the power of gentleness and meekness in diffusing anger and promoting peace. By responding with a gentle and controlled demeanour, we can de-escalate tense situations and create an atmosphere of understanding and resolution.

Humility and meekness also enable us to prioritise the well-being and interests of others. Instead of seeking our own vindication or asserting our rights, we demonstrate a willingness to listen, understand, and empathise with the concerns and perspectives of others. This empathetic approach fosters healthier communication, builds bridges of reconciliation, and promotes mutual respect.

Developing Humility and Meekness: Developing humility and meekness requires intentional effort and reliance on God's transforming power. Here are some practical steps to cultivate these virtues in our lives:

Recognise God's greatness: Regularly reflect on God's majesty, sovereignty, and goodness. Acknowledge His authority over our lives and the privilege of serving Him.

Embrace a servant's heart: Adopt an attitude of service towards others. Look for opportunities to humbly serve and meet the needs of others, following the example of Jesus, who came to serve rather than to be served.

Practice self-examination: Regularly evaluate our motives, attitudes, and actions. Identify areas where pride, self-centeredness, or the desire for control may hinder humility and meekness. Confess and surrender these areas to God, seeking His transformation.

Seek wisdom from the Word of God: Study and meditate on biblical passages that teach about humility and meekness. Allow God's Word to shape our thinking and behaviour, renewing our minds and conforming us to the image of Christ.

Pray for humility and meekness: Humbly ask God to cultivate these virtues. Recognise our dependence on His grace and the work of the Holy Spirit to produce these qualities within us.

Biblical Examples of Humility and Meekness: Throughout the Bible, we find inspiring examples of humility and meekness displayed by individuals who trusted in God and prioritised His will above their own. Some notable examples include:

Moses: Despite his leadership role and close relationship with God, Moses was described as the most humble man on earth (Numbers

12:3). He exhibited meekness in his interactions with the Israelites, interceding for them and seeking God's mercy even when they rebelled against him.

Jesus Christ: The ultimate model of humility and meekness is Jesus Himself. He willingly laid aside His divine privileges and became a servant (Philippians 2:5-8). He demonstrated meekness in His interactions with people, showing compassion, forgiveness, and a gentle spirit even in the face of opposition and injustice.

The Benefits of Humility and Meekness: Embracing humility and meekness in managing anger brings numerous benefits to our lives and relationships:

Improved relationships: Humility and meekness foster healthy and harmonious relationships, creating an atmosphere of understanding, empathy, and mutual respect. They promote effective communication, conflict resolution, and reconciliation.

Emotional well-being: Cultivating humility and meekness helps us let go of pride, ego, and the need to control. It frees us from anger, bitterness, and resentment, leading to greater emotional well-being, peace, and contentment.

Spiritual growth: Humility and meekness are essential for spiritual growth and maturity. They draw us closer to God, allowing His grace to work in and through us. They open our hearts to receive His wisdom, guidance, and transformation.

Humility and meekness are vital virtues in managing anger and cultivating healthy relationships. They enable us to approach anger with a gentle and controlled spirit, prioritising the well-being of others and seeking reconciliation rather than asserting our own rights. By studying and meditating on biblical passages that teach about humility and meekness, we can gain a deeper understanding of God's perspective and the transformative power of these virtues. We can actively develop humility and meekness through prayer, self-examination, and reliance on God's grace.

As we embody these qualities, we reflect the character of Christ, who demonstrated perfect humility and meekness in His earthly ministry. Drawing inspiration from biblical examples such as Moses and Jesus, we can learn to navigate conflicts with grace, extend forgiveness, and promote understanding. The benefits of embracing humility and meekness in anger management include improved relationships, emotional well-being, and spiritual growth.

Let us continually reflect on how we can manifest humility and meekness in our interactions and how these virtues transform our approach to anger and conflict. May we seek God's guidance and rely on His strength to develop a gentle and humble spirit, allowing His transformative work to shape our lives and relationships.

Questions for Reflection

How can I actively cultivate humility and meekness in my interactions with others, especially in moments of anger or conflict?

How can I let go of my ego, pride, and the need to control and instead embrace a gentle and humble spirit that reflects Christ's example?

5.4 Patience and long-suffering

Patience and long-suffering are essential virtues in anger management and maintaining healthy relationships. They allow us to maintain composure, persevere through challenges, and respond to others gracefully and understanding. In this discussion, we will explore the meaning and significance of patience and long-suffering from a biblical perspective, explore relevant passages from the Bible, and reflect on the practical applications of these virtues in our lives.

Understanding Patience and Long-Suffering: Patience can be defined as the ability to remain calm and composed in the face of provocation, delay, or adversity. It involves having a long fuse and not easily succumbing to anger or frustration. On the other hand, long-suffering goes beyond patience and encompasses enduring hardship, injustice, or mistreatment with fortitude and perseverance.

In the Bible, patience and long-suffering are closely linked with the concept of forbearance and are often mentioned together. They reflect a character of steadfastness, endurance, and a willingness to bear with others' faults or offences.

Biblical Examples of Patience and Long-Suffering: Throughout Scripture, we find numerous examples of individuals who exemplified patience and long-suffering. Let's explore a few of these examples:

Job: In the book of Job, we see how Job endured great suffering and loss but remained patient and faithful to God. Despite his friends' misguided counsel and immense trials, Job trusted God's sovereignty and maintained his integrity throughout his ordeal.

Jesus Christ: The ultimate example of patience and long-suffering is found in the life of Jesus. He endured rejection, betrayal, false accusations, and even death on the cross, all for the sake of humanity's salvation. Jesus exhibited unparalleled patience and long-suffering, demonstrating forgiveness and love even in the face of great injustice.

Paul: The apostle Paul endured numerous hardships, including persecution, imprisonment, and physical ailments. Yet, he maintained a patient and long-suffering attitude, trusting in God's grace and relying on His strength to persevere in spreading the gospel.

Biblical Teachings on Patience and Long-Suffering: The Bible contains numerous teachings on the virtues of patience and long-suffering. Let's explore some key passages that provide guidance and inspiration:

James 1:3-4: "Knowing that the testing of your faith produces patience. But let patience have its perfect work, that you may be perfect and complete, lacking nothing." This verse highlights how trials and challenges can produce patience, leading to spiritual growth and maturity.

Colossians 3:12-13: "Therefore, as the elect of God, holy and beloved, put on tender mercies, kindness, humility, meekness, long-suffering; bearing with one another, and forgiving one another, if anyone has a complaint against another; even as Christ forgave you, so you also must do." This passage emphasises the importance of long-suffering in our relationships, encouraging us to bear with one another's faults and extend forgiveness, just as Christ forgave us.

Ephesians 4:2: "With all lowliness and gentleness, with long-suffering, bearing with one another in love." Here, we are urged to demonstrate long-suffering in our interactions, showing patience, understanding, and love towards others.

Galatians 5:22-23: "But the fruit of the Spirit is love, joy, peace, long-suffering, kindness, goodness, faithfulness, gentleness, self-control. Against such, there is no law." This well-known passage in Galatians emphasises that patience and long-suffering require intentional cultivation. They are not always easy to practice, especially in anger or frustration. Still, they play a crucial role in maintaining healthy relationships and reflecting the character of Christ. By studying and meditating on biblical passages that teach about patience and long-suffering, we can gain wisdom and guidance for our own lives.

As we strive to embody these virtues, we must continually reflect on the following questions: How can I cultivate patience in my interactions with others? In what areas of my life do I struggle with long-suffering, and how can I grow? By asking these questions and seeking God's guidance through prayer and study of His Word, we can develop a patient and long-suffering spirit that honours God and positively impacts our relationships.

May we constantly rely on the power of the Holy Spirit to cultivate patience and long-suffering within us, enabling us to navigate conflicts with grace, extend forgiveness, and bear with one another in love. Let us remember the ultimate example of Jesus Christ, who demonstrated perfect patience and long-suffering for our sake and strive to reflect His character in our lives.

Questions for Reflection

In what areas of my life do I struggle with patience and long-suffering the most, and how can I actively cultivate these virtues in those situations?

How does my understanding and practice of patience and long-suffering impact my relationships with others, and what steps can I take to enhance my ability to bear with others in love?

5.5 Love and Compassion

Love and compassion are foundational principles in anger management and in cultivating healthy relationships. These virtues, rooted in the character of God, are vital in navigating conflicts, extending forgiveness, and promoting understanding. In this discussion, we will explore the meaning and significance of love and compassion from a biblical perspective, explore relevant passages from the Bible, and reflect on the practical applications of these virtues in our lives.

The Meaning of Love and Compassion: Love, in the biblical sense, goes beyond mere emotions or feelings. It is an active and sacrificial choice to prioritise the well-being of others, seeking their good above our own. Love is selfless, patient, and kind and seeks to build up and encourage others. Compassion, on the other hand, is the tender-hearted response to the suffering or struggles of others. It involves empathising with others' pain, extending mercy, and offering support and comfort.

In the Bible, love and compassion are closely intertwined and central to God's character. They are exemplified perfectly in the life and ministry of Jesus Christ, who demonstrated unfailing love and compassion towards all people.

Biblical Teachings on Love and Compassion: The Bible contains numerous teachings on the virtues of love and compassion. Let's explore some key passages that provide guidance and inspiration:

1 Corinthians 13:4-7: "Love is patient, love is kind. It does not envy, it does not boast, it is not proud. It does not dishonour others, is not self-seeking, is not easily angered, and keeps no record of wrongs. Love does not delight in evil but rejoices with the truth. It always protects, always trusts, always hopes, always perseveres." This well-known passage in Corinthians gives us a comprehensive understanding of love. It teaches us that love is patient, not easily angered, and it keeps no record of wrongs.

Matthew 22:37-39: "Jesus replied: 'Love the Lord your God with all your heart and soul and mind.' This is the first and greatest commandment. And the second is like it: 'Love your neighbour as yourself.'" Jesus Himself emphasised the centrality of love in our relationship with God and others. He teaches that love for God and our neighbours are the greatest commandments.

Colossians 3:12-14: "Therefore, as God's chosen people, holy and dearly loved, clothe yourselves with compassion, kindness, humility, gentleness, and patience. Bear with each other and forgive one another if any of you has a grievance against someone. Forgive as the Lord forgave you. And over all these virtues put on love, which binds them all together in perfect unity." This passage in Colossians encourages us to clothe ourselves with compassion and love, extending forgiveness and bearing with one another in humility.

Ephesians 4:32: "Be kind and compassionate to one another, forgiving each other, just as in Christ God forgave you." This verse reminds us of the importance of being kind and compassionate, following the example of Christ's forgiveness.

Practical Applications of Love and Compassion: The Bible's teachings on love and compassion have practical implications for our daily lives. Here are some ways we can apply these virtues:

Practice empathy: Seek to understand the perspectives and feelings of others, showing genuine care and concern for their well-being.

Extend forgiveness: Release others from their offences, just as God has forgiven us. Let go of resentment and bitterness and offer grace and reconciliation.

Serve others: Look for opportunities to meet the needs of those around you, whether through acts of kindness, supporting them in their struggles, or lending a listening ear. Show compassion and demonstrate love through tangible actions.

Cultivate a heart of gratitude: Recognise and appreciate your life's blessings and let that overflow into a heart of love and compassion for others. Develop a mindset of thankfulness that leads to generosity and a desire to bless others.

Practice active listening: Show genuine interest in others by listening to their concerns, joys, and struggles. Seek to understand their experiences without judgment or interruption.

Speak encouragement and affirmation: Use your words to build others up, offering words of kindness, encouragement, and affirmation. Let your speech be gracefully seasoned, bringing life and healing to those around you.

Pray for others: Lift up others in prayer, interceding on their behalf. Ask God to grant them strength, healing, and guidance. Pray for wisdom and discernment to best support and love them.

Display patience and gentleness: Cultivate a spirit of patience and gentleness, especially in conflict or disagreement. Let your interactions be characterised by grace, understanding, and a willingness to listen and empathise.

By actively practising love and compassion in our relationships, we reflect the heart of God and create an environment of healing, reconciliation, and harmony. Let us remember the words of Jesus in John 13:34-35: "A new command I give you: Love one another. As I have loved you, so you must love one another. By this, everyone will know you are my disciples if you love one another." Our love and compassion towards others become a testimony of our faith and a reflection of God's love for us.

Love and compassion are essential virtues that should guide our interactions and relationships. Through studying and applying the teachings of the Bible, we gain insights into the depth and significance of these virtues. Let us continually seek to grow in love and compassion, relying on the Holy Spirit to transform our hearts and enable us to love others as Christ loves us. May our lives be a testament to the transformative power of love and compassion, bringing healing, restoration, and the glory of God into the world around us.

Questions for Reflection

How can I actively demonstrate love and compassion in my relationships and interactions with others, even in challenging circumstances?

How can I grow in my understanding and practice of forgiveness, empathy, and kindness towards others, reflecting the love and compassion of Christ?

6. Applying Biblical Wisdom in Conflict Resolution

Conflict is inevitable in human interaction, and navigating and resolving conflicts can greatly impact our relationships and personal well-being. In a world marked by division and strife, followers of Christ need to seek guidance from the Scriptures on approaching conflict with wisdom, grace, and a commitment to reconciliation.

In this chapter, we will explore the invaluable wisdom found in the Bible that can guide us in resolving conflicts and fostering peace in our lives and communities. The Scriptures provide us with principles, examples, and practical advice on how to address conflicts in a manner that reflects the character of God and promotes unity and healing.

Conflict resolution from a biblical perspective goes beyond mere compromise or avoidance. It calls us to embrace a transformative approach that addresses the root causes of conflict, promotes understanding, and restores broken relationships. It requires us to examine our hearts, attitudes, and actions and extend grace and forgiveness to others.

Throughout this chapter, we will explore the rich Bible teachings and how they can be applied to conflict resolution. We will draw insights from the life and ministry of Jesus Christ, who exemplified perfect love, humility, and wisdom in navigating conflicts. We will also learn from the experiences of biblical figures such as Joseph, David, and Paul, who faced various conflicts and demonstrated godly responses.

We will examine specific biblical passages that provide practical guidance on resolving conflicts in a manner that honours God and promotes reconciliation. These teachings include principles of forgiveness, peace-making, communication, humility, and seeking the wisdom of God.

This chapter does not aim to provide a comprehensive guide to conflict resolution, as each situation is unique and may require individualised approaches. Instead, we aim to lay a biblical foundation for understanding conflict resolution, inspire personal reflection, and apply God's principles.

As we explore applying biblical wisdom in conflict resolution, let us approach it with a humble and teachable spirit, recognising that true reconciliation and healing can only come through the power of God's grace. May the insights gleaned from the Scriptures guide us in resolving conflicts with love, wisdom, and a commitment to building bridges of understanding and unity.

"Blessed are the peacemakers, for they shall be called sons of God" (Matthew 5:9, ESV).

Prayer

Gracious and loving God,

We come before You today with hearts open and humble, seeking Your guidance and wisdom in conflict resolution. We thank You for the valuable insights and teachings we have gained from studying Your Word and applying biblical principles to navigate conflicts that reflect Your love and grace.

Lord, we acknowledge that conflicts are an inevitable part of human relationships. They can arise from misunderstandings, differing perspectives, or wounded hearts. We often feel frustrated, hurt, or even angry in these conflicts. But we know, Father, that You have provided us with a roadmap for resolving conflicts to promote understanding, reconciliation, and unity.

We confess, O Lord, that in our human nature, we are prone to respond to conflict with defensiveness, self-righteousness, and a desire to win at all costs. But through Your Word, You call us to a higher standard. You teach us to be peacemakers, seek reconciliation, and extend forgiveness and grace even when difficult.

Father, we ask for Your help applying the biblical wisdom we have learned. Grant us the humility to examine our hearts and attitudes during conflict. Show us any areas where we may contribute to the discord and guide us in making the necessary changes.

Help us to approach conflicts with a spirit of gentleness, seeking first to understand before being understood. Give us the patience to listen attentively, empathise with the feelings and perspectives of others, and communicate with grace and love. Teach us to control our tongues to speak words that bring healing and restoration rather than words that further escalate the conflict.

Lord, we pray for the courage to confront conflicts honestly with humility and respect. Help us to address issues promptly, seeking resolution rather than allowing bitterness and resentment to take root.

Fill us with Your Holy Spirit so that we may respond with wisdom and discernment, knowing when to speak and be silent.

Father, we recognise that true reconciliation often requires forgiveness. Give us the strength to forgive those who have wronged us, just as You have forgiven us through the sacrifice of Your Son, Jesus Christ. Help us to let go of grudges and bitterness and to extend grace and mercy to others as You have extended to us.

We also pray for Your guidance in choosing wise mediators or counsellors when conflicts seem insurmountable. Help us seek godly advice and support from those who can offer wise counsel and help us navigate the complexities of conflict resolution.

Finally, Lord, we ask for Your supernatural peace to reign in our hearts and relationships. May the love and unity we experience in resolving conflicts testify to Your transforming power. Empower us to be instruments of reconciliation and healing in our families, communities, and the world around us.

We offer this prayer in the name of Jesus Christ, who reconciled us to Yourself through His sacrificial love.

Amen.

6.1 Communication Guided by Biblical Principles

Communication is a fundamental aspect of human interaction, and how we communicate can greatly impact our relationships. In anger management, it is crucial to approach communication with wisdom, humility, and love. This section will explore the importance of communication guided by biblical principles, explore relevant Bible passages, and provide practical insights for applying these principles in daily interactions.

The Power of Words: The Bible emphasises the power of our words and their impact on others. Our words have the potential to either build up or tear down, to heal or to hurt. It is important, therefore, to use our words wisely and intentionally, seeking to communicate in a manner that reflects the character of God.

Proverbs 18:21 states, "The tongue has the power of life and death, and those who love it will eat its fruit." This verse highlights the weight and consequences of our words. We can speak life-giving words that encourage, edify, and bring healing or speak words that bring destruction and harm.

Proverbs 15:1 teaches, "A gentle answer turns away wrath, but a harsh word stirs up anger." This verse reminds us of the importance of responding with gentleness and humility, even in conflict or disagreement. By choosing our words carefully, we can diffuse anger and promote understanding.

Biblical Principles for Communication: Speaking Truth in Love: Ephesians 4:15 instructs us to speak the truth in love, emphasising the importance of combining truthfulness with compassion. Communication guided by biblical principles involves speaking honestly and directly but also considering the impact of our words on others' emotions and well-being.

Avoiding Slander and Gossip: Proverbs 20:19 cautions against gossip and spreading slanderous words. Instead, we are encouraged to guard our tongues and speak with integrity. Communication guided by biblical principles involves refraining from engaging in harmful speech and promoting unity and reconciliation.

Active Listening: James 1:19 advises us to be "quick to listen, slow to speak, and slow to become angry." Effective communication involves expressing our thoughts and feelings and actively listening to others. We can foster healthy and respectful dialogue by attentively listening and seeking to understand.

Honouring Others: Romans 12:10 encourages us to "honour one another above yourselves." This means respecting others, valuing their perspectives, and avoiding dismissive or derogatory language. By affirming the dignity and worth of others, we create an environment that fosters healthy and constructive communication.

Practical Application: Cultivate Humility: Communication guided by biblical principles requires humility. Recognise that you may not always have all the answers or a complete understanding of a situation. Be open to learning from others and be willing to admit when you are wrong or have made a mistake.

Choose Words Wisely: Before speaking, take a moment to consider the impact your words may have on others. Ask yourself if your words are necessary, truthful, and spoken lovingly and compassionately. Strive to use words that uplift and encourage others.

Seek Understanding: Instead of assuming or jumping to conclusions, seek to understand the perspectives and feelings of others. Practice active listening, ask clarifying questions, and demonstrate empathy. This not only promotes better communication but also strengthens relationships.

Pray for Guidance: Seek God's guidance and wisdom through prayer before engaging in important or difficult conversations. Ask for His help in choosing the right words, displaying love and understanding, and maintaining a humble and respectful attitude.

Be Willing to Apologise and Forgive: Communication can sometimes be a source of misunderstandings and conflicts. In such situations, it is essential to apologise and seek forgiveness when we have spoken in ways that have caused harm or hurt to others. Ephesians 4:32 reminds us to "be kind to one another, tender-hearted, forgiving one another, as God in Christ forgave you." We can restore broken relationships and promote reconciliation by extending grace and forgiveness.

Communication guided by biblical principles is vital for maintaining healthy and harmonious relationships. By recognising the power of our words, adhering to the biblical principles of speaking the truth in love, avoiding gossip and slander, actively listening, and honouring others, we can foster an environment of understanding, respect, and reconciliation. Applying these principles requires humility, wisdom, and a genuine desire to build others up rather than tear them down.

As we strive to communicate in ways that reflect God's character, let us continually seek His guidance and wisdom through prayer. May our words bring life, healing, and encouragement to those we interact with, and may love, grace, and humility mark our communication. In doing so, we demonstrate the transformative power of biblical communication and contribute to building healthy and thriving relationships.

Questions for Reflection

How can I improve my communication by incorporating the principles of speaking the truth in love, active listening, and honouring others?

Are there any areas in my communication where I need to exercise more humility, wisdom, or restraint to reflect God's character and promote understanding and reconciliation?

6.2 Seeking Reconciliation and Peace-making

Seeking reconciliation and practising peace-making are integral aspects of living out our faith as followers of Christ. In a world filled with conflict and division, the call to pursue reconciliation and promote peace is timely and essential. This section will explore the importance of seeking reconciliation and peace-making, explore relevant Bible passages, and provide practical insights for applying these principles in our daily lives.

The Call to Reconciliation: Reconciliation is at the heart of the gospel message. God, in His infinite love and mercy, initiated reconciliation with humanity through Jesus Christ. As recipients of God's grace and forgiveness, we must extend the same love and reconciliation to others.

2 Corinthians 5:18-19 highlights the central role of reconciliation: "All this is from God, who reconciled us to himself through Christ and gave us the ministry of reconciliation: that God was reconciling the world to himself in Christ, not counting people's sins against them. And he has committed to us the message of reconciliation." As ambassadors of Christ, we are entrusted with the ministry of reconciliation, both in our relationship with God and with others.

Jesus emphasises the importance of reconciliation in Matthew 5:23-24: "Therefore, if you are offering your gift at the altar and there remember that your brother or sister has something against you, leave your gift there in front of the altar. First, go and be reconciled to them; then come and offer your gift." This passage highlights the priority of seeking reconciliation and resolving conflicts before approaching God in worship.

The Practice of Peace-making: Peace-making involves actively working towards peace and fostering harmonious relationships. It requires humility, forgiveness, empathy, and a commitment to seeking the well-being of others. As followers of Christ, we are called to be peacemakers in a world that desperately needs healing and reconciliation.

Jesus blesses peacemakers in Matthew 5:9: "Blessed are the peacemakers, for they will be called children of God." This beatitude highlights the honour and privilege of being peacemakers, as it reflects our identity as children of God. It emphasises the role of peace-making in displaying the character of God and bringing about His kingdom on earth.

Romans 14:19 exhorts believers to "make every effort to do what leads to peace and mutual edification." This verse emphasises the active pursuit of peace for unity and to build up and edify one another.

Practical Application: Self-Reflection and Examination: Begin by examining your own heart and attitudes. Are there any unresolved conflicts or broken relationships that require reconciliation? Pray and ask the Holy Spirit to reveal areas where you need to seek forgiveness or extend forgiveness.

Initiate Reconciliation: Take the initiative to reach out to those with whom you have conflicts or strained relationships. Seek open, honest dialogue opportunities, expressing your desire for reconciliation and healing.

Practice Empathy and Forgiveness: Seek to understand the perspectives and feelings of others involved in conflicts. Cultivate empathy, put yourself in their shoes, and extend forgiveness as Christ has forgiven you (Ephesians 4:32).

Mediation and Reconciliation: In conflicts involving multiple parties, consider involving a neutral mediator or seeking guidance from wise and mature believers within the church community. Their wisdom and guidance can facilitate the process of reconciliation.

Promote Peace in Everyday Interactions: Be intentional about promoting peace in your everyday interactions. Choose words and actions that foster understanding, build bridges, and resolve conflicts rather than escalate them.

The Role of Prayer: Prayer plays a crucial role in seeking reconciliation and practising peace-making. We invite God's wisdom, guidance, and transformative power into our relationships and conflicts through prayer. We can bring our hurts, grievances, and desires for reconciliation before the Lord, seeking His intervention and healing.

Philippians 4:6-7 encourages us to bring our requests to God in prayer: "Do not be anxious about anything, but in every situation, by prayer and petition, with thanksgiving, present your requests to God. And the peace of God, which transcends all understanding, will guard your hearts and minds in Christ Jesus." Prayer opens the door for God's peace to fill our hearts and guide us towards reconciliation.

Matthew 18:19-20 speaks of the power of prayer in conflict resolution: "Again, truly I tell you that if two of you on earth agree about anything they ask for, it will be done for them by my Father in heaven. For where two or three gather in my name, there am I with them." When we gather in prayer, seeking reconciliation and unity, we invite the presence and guidance of Christ into the process.

Seeking reconciliation and practising peace-making are central to our Christian faith. As followers of Christ, we are called to reflect His character by actively pursuing reconciliation, promoting peace, and resolving conflicts. The Bible provides clear guidance and examples of the importance of reconciliation, the practice of peace-making, and the role of prayer in this process.

To apply these principles, we must engage in self-reflection, initiate reconciliation, practice empathy and forgiveness, seek mediation when necessary, and promote peace in our daily interactions. We invite God's transformative power into our relationships through prayer, trusting His guidance and provision.

May we continually strive to be agents of reconciliation and peacemakers, knowing that our efforts contribute to restoring broken relationships, healing wounds, and advancing God's kingdom. Let us remember the words of Jesus in Matthew 5:9, "Blessed are the peacemakers, for they will be called children of God," and seek to embody this calling in every aspect of our lives.

Questions for Reflection

In what areas of my life do I need to actively pursue reconciliation and practice peace-making?

Are any broken relationships or unresolved conflicts requiring my attention and effort?

How can I cultivate a heart of humility, empathy, and forgiveness to become a more effective peacemaker?

How can I promote peace and reconciliation in my interactions with others?

6.3 Responding to Provocation with Grace

Responding to provocation gracefully is a challenging yet essential aspect of our Christian walk. It involves choosing to respond to insults, offences, and hostile behaviour in a manner that reflects the character of Christ. In a world where anger, retaliation, and revenge are often the norm, responding with grace is a testimony to the transformative power of the Holy Spirit within us. This section will explore the importance of responding to provocation with grace, examine relevant passages from the Bible, and provide practical insights for applying this principle in our daily lives.

The Call to Graceful Responses: As followers of Christ, we are called to imitate His character and conduct. This includes responding to provocation in a way that reflects His grace, love, and forgiveness. While our natural inclination may be to respond in kind or seek revenge, the Scriptures call us to a higher standard.

Romans 12:17-21 provides clear guidance on responding to provocation: "Do not repay anyone evil for evil. Be careful to do what is right in the eyes of everyone. If possible, as it depends on you, live at peace with everyone. Do not take revenge, my dear friends, but leave room for God's wrath, for it is written: 'It is mine to avenge; I will repay,' says the Lord. On the contrary: 'If your enemy is hungry, feed him; if thirsty, give him something to drink. In doing this, you will hear burning coals on his head.' Do not be overcome by evil but overcome evil with good." This passage highlights the importance of refraining from retaliating and responding with acts of kindness and love.

Proverbs 15:1 emphasises the impact of our responses: "A gentle answer turns away wrath, but a harsh word stirs up anger." Our words and actions can defuse tense situations and promote peace. Responding with gentleness and kindness can lead to reconciliation and healing.

The Example of Jesus: Jesus exemplified responding to provocation with grace throughout His earthly ministry. Despite facing intense opposition, insults, and persecution, He consistently demonstrated love, forgiveness, and self-control.

In Luke 23:34, even as He was being crucified, Jesus prayed for His enemies: "Father, forgive them, for they do not know what they are doing." This profound act of grace and forgiveness exemplifies Jesus' response to provocation, even in the face of great suffering.

1 Peter 2:23 describes Jesus' response to insults and mistreatment: "When they hurled their insults at him, he did not retaliate; when he suffered, he made no threats. Instead, he entrusted himself to him who judges justly." Jesus trusted in God's justice and did not seek revenge or vindication but instead responded with patience and trust.

Practical Application: Self-Control and Prayer: Cultivate self-control and rely on the power of the Holy Spirit to help you respond to provocation with grace. Seek God's guidance and strength through prayer, asking Him to help you respond in a manner that honours Him.

Reflect and Pause: In moments of provocation, take a moment to pause and reflect before responding. Consider the example of Jesus and ask yourself how He would want you to respond in that situation.

Choose Words Wisely: Proverbs 15:28 advises, "The heart of the righteous weighs its answers, but the mouth of the wicked gushes evil." Choose your words carefully, filling them with grace, kindness, and truth. Avoid engaging in a verbal battle or exchanging insults.

Show Kindness and Love: Responding with grace means demonstrating acts of kindness and love towards those who provoke us. This may involve extending forgiveness, offering a helping hand, or speaking words of encouragement instead of harbouring resentment or seeking retaliation.

Seek Reconciliation: In cases where the provocation stems from a broken relationship, strive for reconciliation and restoration. Matthew

5:23-24 teaches the importance of seeking reconciliation before offering our gifts at the altar: "Therefore if you are offering your gift at the altar and there remember that your brother or sister has something against you, leave your gift there in front of the altar. First, go and be reconciled to them; then come and offer your gift." Actively pursuing reconciliation demonstrates our commitment to responding gracefully and prioritising restoring relationships.

Remember the Greater Purpose: When faced with provocation, remind yourself of the greater purpose of representing Christ in the world. Ephesians 4:29 encourages us to let our words build others up and bring grace to those who hear them. Responding with grace not only reflects our faith but also has the potential to influence others and draw them closer to God.

Responding to provocation gracefully is a challenging yet vital aspect of our Christian journey. It involves imitating Christ's character and choosing to respond in a way that reflects His love, forgiveness, and self-control. Through the power of the Holy Spirit, we can cultivate a heart of grace, seek reconciliation, choose our words wisely, and demonstrate acts of kindness and love. By responding to provocation with grace, we become instruments of peace and witnesses of God's transforming power in our relationships and interactions with others.

Questions for Reflection

In what situations do I find it most challenging to respond to provocation gracefully?

How can I rely on God's strength and the guidance of the Holy Spirit to help me overcome these challenges?

Are there any relationships where I must seek reconciliation and respond to provocation gracefully?

What steps can I take to initiate reconciliation and demonstrate acts of kindness and love?

7. Overcoming Anger Through Faith and Trust

Anger is a powerful emotion that, when left uncontrolled, can wreak havoc on our lives and relationships. It can lead to destructive behaviour, strained connections, and deep inner turmoil. However, as followers of Christ, we are called to a higher standard of living, one that is characterised by love, forgiveness, and self-control. This chapter will explore the transformative power of faith and trust in overcoming anger and cultivating a spirit of peace and reconciliation.

Anger, in its essence, is a response to perceived injustice, hurt, or frustration. It often arises from wounded pride, unmet expectations, or a lack of control over circumstances. While anger is not inherently sinful, how we handle and express it can have profound implications. Fortunately, the Scriptures provide us with guidance and hope, showing us a pathway to overcome anger and embrace a more Christlike response.

In this chapter, we will dive into the depths of God's Word to discover the transformative truths that can help us overcome anger through faith and trust. We will explore the life and teachings of Jesus, who faced provocation and injustice yet responded with grace, wisdom, and self-control. We will also draw wisdom from biblical figures such as Joseph, Moses, and Paul, who navigated challenging situations with faith and reliance on God.

Our journey will take us through key biblical principles and passages that illuminate the path to victory over anger. We will explore the importance of surrendering our will to God, trusting in His sovereignty, and seeking His guidance through prayer and meditation on His Word. We will explore the role of forgiveness, humility, and love in transforming our hearts and responses.

Through personal reflection, practical insights, and scriptural truths, this chapter aims to equip and inspire you to overcome anger through faith and trust in God. It acknowledges that the journey to anger management is not easy or instant. Still, it is possible through the power of the Holy Spirit working within us.

As we embark on this exploration, let us approach it with a spirit of humility, recognising that overcoming anger is a lifelong process that requires daily surrender to God and a genuine desire for transformation. May the insights and wisdom gained from this chapter serve as a roadmap to navigate the challenges of anger, leading us towards a life marked by grace, peace, and a reflection of the character of Christ.

"But the fruit of the Spirit is love, joy, peace, patience, kindness, goodness, faithfulness, gentleness, self-control; against such things, there is no law" (Galatians 5:22-23, ESV).

Prayer

Gracious and loving Father,

We bow before You, acknowledging Your sovereignty and grace. We come to You today seeking divine guidance and intervention as we overcome anger. We thank You for the wisdom and encouragement we have received through studying Your Word and the revelation of Your truth.

Lord, we confess that anger is a powerful emotion that can consume us, cloud our judgment, and hinder our relationships. We recognise that in our own strength, we are powerless to overcome it. But we take comfort in knowing that all things are possible through faith and trust in You.

Father, we surrender our anger and frustrations into Your loving hands. We ask Your Holy Spirit to work in our hearts, transforming our attitudes and helping us respond with grace, patience, and love. Teach us to rely on You completely, to trust in Your unfailing wisdom, and to lean on Your strength when our own fail us.

Help us to release our grip on control and surrender our desires and expectations to Your perfect will. Remind us that You control every situation and that Your plans are higher and wiser than our own. Give us the faith to trust that You are working all things together for our good, even in challenging circumstances.

Lord, we pray for discernment to identify the root causes of our anger. Show us any unresolved pain, past hurts, or unmet needs that may fuel our anger. Heal our wounded hearts and fill us with Your peace, enabling us to forgive those who wronged us and let go of grudges and bitterness.

Teach us to pause and reflect before reacting in anger. Grant us the wisdom to choose our words and actions carefully, ensuring they align with Your truth and grace. Help us respond with love and kindness, even when provoked or mistreated. Fill us with Your Spirit, that we may bear the fruits of patience, self-control, and gentleness.

Father, we pray for the strength to resist the temptations that lead to anger. Guard our hearts and minds against the influences of this world that fuel anger and hostility. Help us to set healthy boundaries, to practice self-care, and to seek healthy outlets for our emotions.

We also pray for accountability and support. Surround us with wise and faithful friends and mentors who will lovingly encourage and challenge us to overcome anger. Give us the humility to seek help and the willingness to engage in counselling or therapy if necessary for our healing and growth.

Above all, Lord, we ask for Your grace to transform us from the inside out. Mould us into vessels of Your love, peace, and forgiveness. May our lives be a testimony of Your transformative power, reflecting the image of Christ to the world.

We offer this prayer in the name of Jesus Christ, our Savior and Redeemer, who conquered sin and anger through His perfect sacrifice.

Amen.

7.1 Trusting in God's Plan and Sovereignty

Trusting in God's plan and sovereignty is fundamental to our faith journey. It involves acknowledging God's wisdom, power, and authority over all things and surrendering our lives and circumstances to His control. This section will explore the significance of trusting in God's plan and sovereignty, examine relevant Bible passages, and draw practical insights for applying this trust in our daily lives.

The Nature of God's Plan and Sovereignty: God's Omniscience: God possesses perfect knowledge and understanding of all things, including the past, present, and future. Isaiah 46:10 affirms, "I make known the end from the beginning, from ancient times, what is still to come. I say, 'My purpose will stand, and I will do all that I please.'" This verse assures us that God's plan is rooted in His perfect knowledge, and nothing surprises Him.

God's Sovereignty: God exercises supreme authority and control over the universe. Psalm 103:19 declares, "The Lord has established his throne in heaven, and his kingdom rules overall." God's sovereignty means that He governs all things according to His purposes, and nothing happens outside His divine will.

Trusting in God's Plan and Sovereignty: Proverbs 3:5- 6 offers guidance on trusting God: "Trust in the Lord with all your heart and lean not on your own understanding; in all your ways submit to him, and he will make your paths straight." This passage encourages us to trust God, even when we don't fully comprehend His ways or our circumstances.

Romans 8:28 assures us of God's purpose in everything: "And we know that in all things God works for the good of those who love him, who have been called according to his purpose." Even during challenges, setbacks, or trials, we can trust that God is working out His good purposes and will ultimately bring about good from every situation.

Practical Application: Seeking God's Guidance: Trusting in God's plan and sovereignty begins with seeking His guidance and wisdom. Proverbs 16:3 advises, "Commit to the Lord whatever you do, and he will establish your plans." Involve God in decision-making, seek His will through prayer and Scripture, and trust His leading.

Surrendering Control: Trusting in God's plan requires letting go of our desire for control and surrendering to His greater wisdom and authority. Psalm 46:10 encourages us to "Be still and know that I am God." Recognise that God's ways are higher than ours (Isaiah 55:8-9) and that He can orchestrate our lives according to His plan.

Resting in God's Promises: Hold onto the promises of God's faithfulness and goodness, even when circumstances seem uncertain. Psalm 119:105 assures us, "Your word is a lamp for my feet, a light on my path." Meditate on God's Word, reminding yourself of His past faithfulness, and allow His promises to anchor your trust in His plan.

Developing a Faith-Filled Perspective: Cultivate a faith-filled perspective that sees beyond the present circumstances. 2 Corinthians 4:18 encourages us, "So we fix our eyes not on what is seen, but on what is unseen since what is seen is temporary, but what is unseen is eternal." Trusting in God's plan requires looking beyond the temporary and placing our hope in the eternal purposes of God.

Embracing Peace and Contentment: Philippians 4:6-7 reminds us of the peace that comes from trusting in God's plan and sovereignty: "Do not be anxious about anything, but in every situation, by prayer and petition, with thanksgiving, present your requests to God. And the peace of God, which transcends all understanding, will guard your hearts and minds in Christ Jesus." When we trust in God's plan, we can experience a deep sense of peace that surpasses human understanding.

Jeremiah 29:11 assures us of God's good plans for us: "For I know the plans I have for you," declares the Lord, "plans to prosper you and not to harm you, plans to give you hope and a future." This verse reminds us that God's plans are ultimately for our well-being and future hope.

Trusting in God's plan and sovereignty is essential to our faith. It requires surrendering our control, seeking God's guidance, and embracing His promises. We can experience peace, contentment, and hope even in uncertainty as we trust His perfect wisdom and authority.

Questions for Reflection

How can I actively surrender control and trust God's plan and sovereignty?

Are there areas in my life where I struggle to trust God's plan?

How can I lean on His promises and seek guidance in those areas?

7.2 Overcoming Anger Through Faith

Overcoming anger through faith is important to personal growth and spiritual maturity. If left unchecked, anger can destroy our well-being and relationships. In this section, we will explore the biblical perspective on anger, the role of faith in managing and overcoming anger, and practical steps to cultivate a spirit of peace and self-control.

The Nature of Anger: Ephesians 4:26-27 provides insights into anger: "In your anger do not sin: Do not let the sun go down while you are still angry, and do not give the devil a foothold." This passage acknowledges that anger is a natural emotion. Still, it emphasises handling it appropriately and avoiding letting it lead to sin.

Proverbs 14:29 highlights the importance of self-control concerning anger: "Whoever is patient has great understanding, but one who is quick-tempered displays folly." This verse encourages us to cultivate patience and self-control while navigating situations that may trigger our anger.

The Role of Faith in Overcoming Anger: Galatians 5:22-23 describes the fruit of the Spirit, which includes self-control: "But the fruit of the Spirit is love, joy, peace, forbearance, kindness, goodness, faithfulness, gentleness and self-control. Against such things, there is no law." Faith in God empowers us to exhibit the fruit of the Spirit, including self-control, which is crucial in managing and overcoming anger.

James 1:19-20 provides valuable wisdom on handling anger: "My dear brothers and sisters, take note of this: Everyone should be quick to listen, slow to speak and slow to become angry because human anger does not produce the righteousness that God desires." This passage emphasises the importance of self-control and the practice of listening and speaking with wisdom to avoid uncontrolled anger.

Practical Steps for Overcoming Anger through Faith: Surrender to God: Recognise that anger is a natural emotion, but surrender it to

God, seeking His guidance and strength to respond in a way that aligns with His will. Proverbs 3:5-6 reminds us, "Trust in the LORD with all your heart and lean not on your own understanding; in all your ways submit to him, and he will make your paths straight."

Seek God's Perspective: When anger rises, pause and seek God's perspective. Proverbs 19:11 advises, "A person's wisdom yields patience; it is to one's glory to overlook an offence." By seeking God's wisdom and guidance, we can gain a broader perspective that helps us respond with patience and understanding.

Practice Forgiveness: Unforgiveness is often at the root of unresolved anger. Ephesians 4:31-32 instructs us, "Get rid of all bitterness, rage, and anger, brawling and slander, along with every malice. Be kind and compassionate to one another, forgiving each other, just as in Christ God forgave you." By extending forgiveness to those who have wronged us, we release the hold of anger and make room for healing and reconciliation.

Renew the Mind: Transforming our thinking is crucial in overcoming anger. Romans 12:2 encourages us, "Do not conform to the pattern of this world but be transformed by renewing your mind. Then you can test and approve God's will—his good, pleasing and perfect will." By immersing ourselves in God's Word, meditating on His truth, and aligning our thoughts with His principles, we can experience a renewal of our minds and a transformation in our responses to anger.

Seek Accountability and Support: Surround yourself with a community of believers who can provide support, encouragement, and accountability in managing anger. Proverbs 27:17 states, "As iron sharpens iron, so one person sharpens another." Having trusted individuals who hold us accountable and provide wise counsel can help us navigate anger healthily and constructively.

Practice Gratitude and Worship: Cultivating a heart of gratitude and engaging in worship can shift our focus away from anger and toward God's goodness and faithfulness. Psalm 100:4 reminds us,

"Enter his gates with thanksgiving and his courts with praise; give thanks to him and praise his name." As we redirect our attention to God's blessings and worship Him, our hearts are filled with peace and joy, diminishing the power of anger.

Overcoming anger through faith is a transformative journey that requires surrender, seeking God's perspective, practising forgiveness, renewing our minds, and seeking support from a community of believers. Through the power of the Holy Spirit and the application of biblical principles, we can develop a spirit of self-control, patience, and love, allowing our faith to shape our responses to anger.

Questions for Reflection

How can I surrender my anger to God and seek His guidance?

What practical steps can I take to renew my mind and align my thoughts with God's truth when anger arises?

7.3 Developing Resilience and Reliance on God

Resilience and reliance on God are vital to navigating life's challenges and overcoming adversity. This section will explore the biblical perspective on resilience, the importance of relying on God, and practical steps to develop resilience and deepen our trust in Him.

The Nature of Resilience: Resilience can be defined as the ability to bounce back from difficulties, setbacks, and hardships. It involves having a strong and flexible mindset, unwavering faith, and a firm reliance on God's guidance and strength. While "resilience" may not be explicitly mentioned in the Bible, its principles and characteristics are found throughout Scripture.

James 1:2-4 teaches us about the role of trials in developing resilience: "Consider it pure joy, my brothers and sisters, whenever you face trials of many kinds because you know that the testing of your faith produces perseverance. Let perseverance finish its work so you may be mature and complete, not lacking anything." This passage highlights the connection between trials, perseverance, and character development.

Romans 5:3-4 reinforces that trials produce resilience: "Not only so, but we also glory in our sufferings, because we know that suffering produces perseverance; perseverance, character; and character, hope." We develop resilience and character through enduring hardships and relying on God's strength.

Relying on God's Strength: Philippians 4:13 declares, "I can do all this through him who gives me strength." This verse reminds us that our strength comes from God. When we face challenges, we can lean on His power, wisdom, and grace to overcome them. Relying on God acknowledges our dependence on Him and recognises He is the ultimate source of strength.

Psalm 46:1 assures us of God's presence and help in times of trouble: "God is our refuge and strength, an ever-present help in trouble." This verse reminds us that God is with us and will provide the strength to persevere and overcome difficulties.

Developing Resilience and Reliance on God: Trust in God's Promises: Throughout the Bible, God provides numerous promises of His faithfulness, provision, and guidance. By studying and meditating on these promises, we can build trust in Him and develop resilience. One such promise is found in Isaiah 41:10, where God says, "So do not fear, for I am with you; do not be dismayed, for I am your God. I will strengthen, help, and uphold you with my righteous right hand."

Prayer and Seeking God's Guidance: A prayer is a powerful tool for developing resilience and reliance on God. Through prayer, we express our dependence on Him, seek His wisdom, and find comfort in His presence. Philippians 4:6-7 encourages us, "Do not be anxious about anything, but in every situation, by prayer and petition, with thanksgiving, present your requests to God. And the peace of God, which transcends all understanding, will guard your hearts and minds in Christ Jesus."

Embracing God's Sovereignty: Resilience is fostered when we trust in God's sovereignty, knowing He is in control of all things, even during challenges. Romans 8:28 assures us, "And we know that in all things God works for the good of those who love him, who have been called according to his purpose." Even in difficult circumstances, we can find comfort in knowing God works for our good and His purposes.

Learning from Biblical Examples: The Bible is replete with examples of individuals who demonstrated resilience and reliance on God in the face of adversity. The stories of Joseph, Job, David, and Paul are just a few among many.

Joseph faced betrayal by his brothers, slavery, and imprisonment, yet he remained steadfast in his faith and trust in God. Despite his circumstances, Joseph acknowledged God's sovereignty and believed that God had a purpose for his life. Ultimately, God elevated Joseph to great authority and used him to save his family and the nation of Egypt (Genesis 37-50).

Job experienced unimaginable loss and suffering, yet he refused to curse God or turn away from Him. Instead, he maintained his trust in God's wisdom and sovereignty, declaring, "Naked I came from my mother's womb, and naked I will depart. The LORD gave, and the LORD has taken away; may the name of the LORD be praised" (Job 1:21). During his trials, Job clung to his faith and found restoration and blessing in the end (Job 42).

David, the renowned psalmist and king of Israel, faced numerous challenges and enemies throughout his life. However, he consistently turned to God for strength and guidance. In Psalm 23, David expresses his unwavering trust in God as his shepherd, saying, "Even though I walk through the darkest valley, I will fear no evil, for you are with me; your rod and your staff, they comfort me" (Psalm 23:4). David's reliance on God sustained him through difficult times and brought him victory.

The apostle Paul endured persecution, imprisonment, and numerous hardships for the gospel's sake. Yet, he maintained a deep faith and dependence on God. In his letter to the Philippians, Paul writes, "I can do all this through him who gives me strength" (Philippians 4:13). Despite his challenges, Paul relied on God's power and grace to sustain him and fulfil his purpose.

From these examples and many others, we learn that developing resilience and reliance on God requires:

- Trusting in God's faithfulness and promises, even in difficulties.
- Seeking God's guidance and strength through prayer.
- We should embrace God's sovereignty and believe He is working on everything for our good.

- Learning from the stories of faithful individuals in the Bible who demonstrated resilience and reliance on God.
- Surrounding ourselves with a supportive community of believers who can encourage and uplift us in our journey.

In developing resilience and reliance on God, we must remember that it is a lifelong process. It requires daily surrender, intentional faith, and a willingness to persevere through trials. As we deepen our trust in God and lean on Him for strength, we can face adversity confidently, knowing He is our source of hope and victory.

Developing resilience and reliance on God is essential for navigating life's challenges. We can cultivate resilience and deepen our reliance on God through trust in God's promises, prayer, embracing His sovereignty, learning from biblical examples, and seeking support from the faith community.

Questions for Reflection

How can I cultivate a deeper trust in God's faithfulness and promises in difficulties?

What practical steps can I take to rely more fully on God's strength and guidance daily?

8. Restorative Justice and Forgiveness

In a broken and hurting world, restorative justice and forgiveness hold tremendous power to heal wounds, restore relationships, and bring about transformative change. The human experience is riddled with pain, conflict, and injustice, and our natural inclination is often to seek retribution or hold on to bitterness and resentment. However, as followers of Christ, we are called to a different path that leads to reconciliation, restoration, and the transformative power of forgiveness.

This chapter explores the profound and challenging topics of restorative justice and forgiveness, drawing from biblical wisdom and teachings. We will explore the transformative nature of forgiveness and its role in releasing the burdens of anger, bitterness, and unforgiveness. We will also explore restorative justice principles and practices, which seek to repair the harm caused by wrongdoing and promote healing for all parties involved.

Throughout history, we find stories of individuals who have embraced the power of forgiveness, from Joseph, who forgave his brothers despite their betrayal, to Jesus Christ Himself, who extended forgiveness even while hanging on the cross. These examples serve as beacons of hope, showing us that forgiveness is possible and a profound act of obedience to God's commandments.

This chapter will explore the biblical foundations of forgiveness and restorative justice, examining key passages illuminating these principles' transformative power. We will also address the misconceptions and challenges surrounding these concepts, providing practical insights and guidance for navigating the complexities of forgiveness and seeking restoration.

Our journey will take us through the steps of forgiveness, highlighting the importance of acknowledging pain, extending grace, and letting go of resentment. We will also explore the process of reconciliation, emphasising the need for empathy, active listening, and a commitment to understanding the perspectives of others.

It is important to recognise that embracing restorative justice and forgiveness does not mean dismissing or minimising the harm caused by wrongdoing. Instead, it acknowledges the reality of brokenness and seeks a path towards healing, growth, and restoration. It invites individuals and communities to unite in love and compassion, fostering environments where justice and mercy intertwine.

As we embark on this exploration, may our hearts be open to the transformative power of forgiveness and restorative justice. May we be inspired by the example of Christ, who forgave us when we were undeserving, and may His grace flow through us as we extend forgiveness to others. May this chapter serve as a guide, equipping us to navigate the complexities of forgiveness and embrace a journey of healing, reconciliation, and restoration.

"Be kind to one another, tender-hearted, forgiving one another, as God in Christ forgave you" (Ephesians 4:32, ESV).

Prayer

Gracious and merciful God,

We come before You humbly, acknowledging Your perfect justice and abundant grace. We thank You for the profound revelation of restorative justice and forgiveness in Your Word. As we reflect on the truths shared in this chapter, we are reminded of Your infinite capacity to heal, restore, and reconcile.

Father, we confess that forgiveness can be a daunting and challenging task. Our human nature often clings to pain, resentment, and a desire for revenge. But through Your Word, You have shown us the path of forgiveness and the freedom it brings. You have called us to be agents of reconciliation and peacemakers in a broken world.

Today, we lay our hurts, grievances, and deep-seated wounds before You. We release them into Your hands, knowing that Your justice is perfect and Your ways are higher than ours. Help us to trust in Your wisdom and guidance as we navigate the difficult journey of forgiveness.

Lord, we recognise that forgiveness does not mean condoning or forgetting the offences committed against us. It is a choice to surrender the burden of anger and bitterness to Your care. Grant us the strength to extend grace and mercy, just as You have extended it to us through the sacrifice of Your Son, Jesus Christ.

In the process of forgiveness, we also acknowledge the need for healing. Heal our wounded hearts and restore our broken relationships. Help us to seek reconciliation whenever possible, pursuing peace and unity with those who have caused us pain. Give us the wisdom to set healthy boundaries and the courage to engage in honest and loving conversations that promote understanding and healing.

Father, we pray for the grace to forgive ourselves. Often, we carry guilt and shame for the harm we have caused others or the mistakes we have made. We ask for Your forgiveness and the strength to forgive ourselves, knowing that Your grace covers all our shortcomings.

In this restorative justice and forgiveness journey, we also recognise the power of empathy and compassion. Help us see others through Your eyes and understand their struggles and brokenness. May our hearts be filled with love and compassion, leading us to extend forgiveness even when it seems impossible.

Lord, we commit ourselves to walk according to Your command to forgive. Help us to remember the example of Christ, who forgave those who crucified Him, saying, "Father, forgive them, for they know not what they do" (Luke 23:34). May His sacrificial love inspire us to forgive as we have been forgiven.

We thank You, Lord, for the transformative power of forgiveness. We pray that Your Holy Spirit will empower us to live as peace, reconciliation, and restoration instruments. May our lives reflect Your grace and forgiveness, drawing others to the abundant life found in You.

We pray in the name of Jesus, the ultimate example of forgiveness.

Amen.

8.1 Understanding Biblical Principles of Justice

Justice is a fundamental aspect of God's character and a central theme throughout the Bible. It encompasses fairness, righteousness, and establishing order and equity in society. In understanding biblical principles of justice, we will explore the biblical foundation of justice, God's call for justice, and the implications of justice in our lives.

The Biblical Foundation of Justice: The Bible consistently emphasises the importance of justice. God's character as a just and righteous God is revealed from the Old Testament to the New Testament. In Deuteronomy 32:4, it is stated, "He is the Rock, his works are perfect, and all his ways are just. A faithful God who does no wrong, upright and just is he." This verse highlights God's unwavering commitment to justice and His perfect nature.

Psalm 89:14 declares, "Righteousness and justice are the foundation of your throne; love and faithfulness go before you." This verse emphasises the inseparable connection between God's justice and His righteousness. God's justice is grounded in His righteous character and is the foundation upon which His reign is established.

God's Call for Justice: Throughout Scripture, God calls His people to practice justice in their dealings with others. In the book of Micah, the prophet emphasises the importance of justice when he says, "He has shown you, O mortal, what is good. And what does the Lord require of you? To act justly and to love mercy and to walk humbly with your God" (Micah 6:8). This verse encapsulates God's expectation for His people to actively pursue justice, show compassion, and maintain a humble relationship with Him.

In the New Testament, Jesus affirms the significance of justice. In Matthew 23:23, He criticises the Pharisees for neglecting justice, mercy, and faithfulness, stating, "Woe to you, teachers of the law and

Pharisees, you hypocrites! You give a tenth of your spices—mint, dill, and cumin. But you have neglected the more important matters of the law—justice, mercy, and faithfulness. You should have practised the latter without neglecting the former." Jesus' words emphasise the priority of justice and its inseparable connection to mercy and faithfulness.

Implications of Justice in Our Lives: Understanding biblical principles of justice has significant implications for our lives and interactions with others. It calls us to treat all individuals with fairness, dignity, and respect, regardless of their social status, ethnicity, or background. It challenges us to stand against oppression, inequality, and any form of injustice in society.

Justice demands that we advocate for the vulnerable, the marginalised, and the oppressed. Proverbs 31:8-9 states, "Speak up for those who cannot speak for themselves, for the rights of all destitute. Speak up and judge fairly; defend the rights of the poor and needy." This verse highlights our responsibility to use our voice and resources to seek justice for those who cannot do so themselves.

Justice compels us to actively address systemic issues and work towards societal transformation. Isaiah 1:17 says, "Learn to do right; seek justice. Defend the oppressed. Take up the fatherless's cause; plead the widow's case." This verse highlights the call to seek justice and actively engage in actions that bring about positive change and alleviate the suffering of others.

In our personal lives, understanding biblical principles of justice prompts us to examine our attitudes, prejudices, and actions. It challenges us to confront any biases or injustices within ourselves and work towards personal transformation in alignment with God's standards of justice. It requires us to cultivate a heart of compassion, humility, and a commitment to seek reconciliation and restoration.

Understanding biblical principles of justice is crucial for followers of Christ. It provides a foundation for our interactions with others, our pursuit of righteousness, and our commitment to social transformation. God's call for justice resonates throughout the pages of Scripture, reminding us of His unwavering commitment to righteousness and equity. As we align ourselves with His character and seek to practice justice in our lives, we become agents of His kingdom, working towards a world where justice flows like a mighty river.

Questions for Reflection

In what areas of my life do I struggle to uphold biblical principles of justice?

How can I actively work towards aligning my thoughts, words, and actions with God's standards of justice?

Am I using my voice and influence to speak up against injustice and advocate for the oppressed?

How can I more effectively engage in bringing about positive change in my community and society as a whole?

8.2 The Role of Forgiveness in Healing and Reconciliation

Forgiveness plays a vital role in healing and reconciliation, both in our relationship with God and in interactions with others. It is a powerful and transformative act that has the potential to mend broken relationships, bring inner healing, and restore peace. In this discussion, we will explore the biblical perspective on forgiveness, the benefits of forgiveness, and the practical implications of forgiveness in the context of healing and reconciliation.

The Biblical Perspective on Forgiveness: The Bible presents forgiveness as a central theme throughout its pages. It highlights God's forgiveness towards humanity and calls us to emulate His example in extending forgiveness to others. Ephesians 4:32 says, "Be kind and compassionate to one another, forgiving each other, just as in Christ God forgave you." This verse emphasises the mandate for believers to forgive others as God has forgiven them.

Jesus teaches about the importance of forgiveness in the Lord's Prayer: "And forgive us our debts, as we also have forgiven our debtors" (Matthew 6:12). This prayer reveals the reciprocal nature of forgiveness. As we receive forgiveness from God, we are called to extend forgiveness to those who have wronged us.

The Benefits of Forgiveness: Forgiveness brings numerous benefits to both the forgiver and the forgiven. It is a transformative act that releases anger, resentment, and bitterness. Through forgiveness, we experience emotional healing and freedom. Proverbs 14:30 states, "A heart at peace gives life to the body, but envy rots the bones." Forgiveness brings peace to our hearts, leading to overall well-being and restoration.

Forgiveness also fosters reconciliation. It opens the door for restored relationships, bridging the gap between individuals divided by hurt and offence. In Matthew 5:23-24, Jesus teaches the importance of reconciling with others before offering our gifts to God, emphasising the significance of restored relationships in our worship and spiritual life.

Practical Implications of Forgiveness in Healing and Reconciliation: Healing: Forgiveness is a powerful tool in the healing process. It enables individuals to release the pain of past offences and move forward with renewed hope and joy. Psalm 147:3 affirms God's role in healing our wounds: "He heals the broken-hearted and binds up their wounds." As we forgive others, we align ourselves with God's healing work, allowing Him to mend our broken hearts.

Reconciliation: Forgiveness is a crucial step towards reconciliation. It opens the door for dialogue, understanding, and restoration of trust. In Matthew 18:15, Jesus instructs us on resolving conflicts within the Christian community, highlighting the importance of seeking reconciliation rather than harbouring grudges or seeking revenge. Forgiveness paves the way for reconciliation, where broken relationships can be restored and renewed.

Letting go of the past: Forgiveness enables us to let go of the past and embrace a future filled with hope and freedom. Philippians 3:13-14 encourages us to forget what lies behind us and press on toward the goal of our upward calling in Christ Jesus. By forgiving, we release ourselves from the grip of the past and open ourselves up to new opportunities for growth, love, and reconciliation.

Reflecting God's character: Forgiveness allows us to reflect on His character and love for humanity. In Colossians 3:13, Paul instructs believers to "bear with each other and forgive one another if any of you has a grievance against someone. Forgive as the Lord forgave you." As we forgive, we display God's mercy, grace, and unconditional love to those around us, becoming agents of reconciliation and ambassadors of Christ's love.

The Challenges and Rewards of Forgiveness: While forgiveness is a powerful and transformative act, it is not always easy to practice. It can be challenging to let go of the pain and hurt caused by others, especially in cases of deep betrayal or trauma. However, the rewards of forgiveness far outweigh the difficulties.

Inner Freedom: Forgiveness brings inner freedom and liberation from resentment and anger. It allows us to release the negative emotions that can weigh us down and hinder our personal growth and well-being.

Restoration of Relationships: Forgiveness opens the door for restoring broken relationships. It paves the way for reconciliation, creating the possibility for healing and renewed connections with others.

Spiritual Growth: Forgiveness is a vital aspect of spiritual growth. It deepens our relationship with God as we align our hearts with His heart of forgiveness and mercy. Through forgiveness, we become more Christlike, embodying His love and grace in our interactions with others.

Healing Communities: Practicing forgiveness brings healing on an individual level and contributes to healing within communities and society. When individuals choose to forgive, it can lead to a ripple effect, fostering a culture of reconciliation, peace, and justice.

Examples of Forgiveness in the Bible: The Bible provides numerous examples of forgiveness, illustrating its transformative power and impact. One powerful example is the story of Joseph in the Book of Genesis. Despite being betrayed by his brothers, Joseph forgave them and ultimately reconciled with them (Genesis 50:15-21). His act of forgiveness restored the relationship with his family. It brought about the preservation and blessing of the entire Israelite nation.

Another notable example is Jesus on the cross, who forgave those who crucified Him, saying, "Father, forgive them, for they do not know what they are doing" (Luke 23:34). This ultimate act of forgiveness demonstrates the depth of God's love and His desire for reconciliation with humanity.

Practical Steps Towards Forgiveness: Acknowledge the pain: Recognise and acknowledge the pain caused by the offence. Valuing your emotions and seeking support through prayer, counselling, or trusted individuals is essential.

Choose forgiveness: Make a deliberate choice to forgive, releasing the person from the debt they owe you. This choice does not necessarily condone or excuse the offence but seeks healing and reconciliation.

Seek God's help: Pray for God's grace and strength to forgive. Surrender your pain and hurt to Him, allowing His love and healing to work in your heart.

Renew your mind: Replace negative thoughts and emotions with positive and compassionate ones. Meditate on God's Word and align your thoughts with His perspective on forgiveness.

Extend forgiveness: Consider extending forgiveness directly to the person who hurt you, if possible and appropriate. Alternatively, release the offence to God and commit to praying for the person's well-being and transformation.

Embrace healing: Engage in self-care, seek healing through counselling or support groups, and surround yourself with a community that fosters forgiveness, healing, and growth.

The Ultimate Example: God's Forgiveness: The ultimate example of forgiveness is found in God's forgiveness towards humanity. Romans 5:8 states, "But God demonstrates his love for us in this: While we were still sinners, Christ died for us." God's unconditional forgiveness is offered to all who repent and turn to Him.

As recipients of God's forgiveness, we are called to extend the same grace and forgiveness to others. Ephesians 4:32 reminds us, "Be kind and compassionate to one another, forgiving each other, just as in Christ God forgave you."

Forgiveness plays a crucial role in healing and reconciliation. It is a transformative act that brings freedom, restoration, and spiritual growth. By following the biblical principles of forgiveness, we reflect the character of God and become agents of reconciliation in our relationships and communities. Forgiveness may be challenging, but the rewards of inner freedom, restored relationships, and spiritual growth outweigh the difficulties. Through the examples of forgiveness in the Bible and the guidance of God's Word, we are empowered to choose forgiveness, seek reconciliation, and experience the profound healing and transformative power that comes from extending and receiving forgiveness.

Questions for Reflection

Is there anyone I need to forgive or seek forgiveness from?

How can I take steps towards reconciliation and healing in those relationships?

How can I further cultivate a lifestyle of forgiveness and extend grace and compassion to others, reflecting the character of God in my interactions and relationships?

8.3 Seeking Restoration and Making Amends

Seeking restoration and making amends are important aspects of healing, reconciliation, and living out the principles of forgiveness. When we recognise that our actions have caused harm or when we have been on the receiving end of someone else's wrongdoing, seeking restoration and making amends allows for the repair and rebuilding of relationships and the opportunity for personal growth and transformation. This section will explore the biblical perspective on seeking restoration and making amends and how it can contribute to healing and reconciliation.

The Biblical Foundation of Restoration and Making Amends: The Bible emphasises the importance of seeking restoration and making amends in relationships. It recognises that our actions have consequences and calls us to take responsibility for our behaviour and actively work towards reconciliation and restoration.

The Call to Reconciliation: In several passages, the Bible calls believers to seek reconciliation and make amends. In Matthew 5:23-24, Jesus instructs his followers, "So if you are offering your gift at the altar and there remember that your brother has something against you, leave your gift there before the altar and go. First, be reconciled to your brother, and then come and offer your gift." This teaches us that seeking reconciliation and making amends take precedence over religious rituals.

Restoring Broken Relationships: The Bible encourages believers to restore broken relationships and mend the damage caused by wrongdoing. Galatians 6:1-2 says, "Brothers and sisters if someone is caught in a sin, you who live by the Spirit should restore that person gently. But watch yourselves, or you also may be tempted. Carry each other's burdens, and in this way, you will fulfil the law of Christ." This passage highlights the importance of restoring others gently, offering support and bearing each other's burdens.

Making Amends: Making amends involves taking tangible actions to repair the harm caused. In Luke 19:8, Zacchaeus, a tax collector, demonstrates this principle when he encounters Jesus. He says, "Behold, Lord, the half of my goods I give to the poor. And if I have defrauded anyone of anything, I restore it fourfold." Zacchaeus's response exemplifies the desire to make amends by going beyond mere restitution and seeking to make things right by going above and beyond what is required.

The Process of Seeking Restoration and Making Amends: Acknowledgment of Wrongdoing: The first step in seeking restoration and making amends is acknowledging our wrongdoing. This involves taking responsibility for our actions, admitting the harm caused, and recognising the impact on others.

Genuine Repentance: Repentance is a key component of seeking restoration. It goes beyond mere remorse and involves a sincere desire to change and turn away from our harmful behaviours. Psalm 51:17 states, "The sacrifices of God are a broken spirit; a broken and contrite heart, O God, you will not despise." A humble and contrite heart opens the door to true repentance.

Seeking Forgiveness: In seeking restoration, we must humbly approach the harmed person and ask for forgiveness. Matthew 5:23-24 instructs us to seek reconciliation with others before presenting our gifts to God. This demonstrates the priority of restoring relationships and making amends.

Restitution and Repair: Making amends may involve taking practical steps to repair the harm caused. This could include restitution, compensating for losses, or actively working towards rectifying the consequences of our actions. It requires a commitment to doing what is necessary to restore trust and heal the relationship.

Transformation and Growth: Seeking Restoration and making amends benefit the individuals involved and contribute to personal growth and transformation. It requires a willingness to learn from our mistakes, develop empathy, and cultivate a character that reflects Christ's love and grace.

The Healing Power of Restoration and Making Amends: Reconciliation and Healing: Seeking restoration and making amends pave the way for relationship reconciliation and healing. James 5:16 says, "Therefore, confess your sins to one another and pray for one another, that you may be healed." By taking steps towards reconciliation and making amends, we create an environment where forgiveness, healing, and restoration can occur.

Freedom from Guilt and Regret: Making amends allows us to address the guilt and regret that weigh heavily on our hearts. 2 Corinthians 7:10 states, "For godly grief produces a repentance that leads to salvation without regret, whereas worldly grief produces death." By actively seeking restoration and making amends, we can experience the freedom from reconciling with others and finding peace within ourselves.

Witnessing God's Grace: When we demonstrate a commitment to seeking restoration and making amends, we witness God's grace and redemption. Our actions reflect God's character and the transformative power of His love. Ephesians 4:32 reminds us, "Be kind to one another, tender-hearted, forgiving one another, as God in Christ forgave you."

Challenges and Considerations: Willingness of the Other Party: Seeking restoration and making amends requires both parties' willingness. While we can take responsibility for our actions, we cannot control the response or actions of others. It is important to respect their boundaries and timing and to be prepared for different outcomes.

Continual Growth and Learning: The journey of seeking restoration and making amends is ongoing. It requires humility, self-reflection, and a commitment to growth. We may encounter setbacks and challenges along the way. Still, through perseverance and reliance on God's guidance, we can continue to mature in our ability to seek restoration and make amends.

The Impact of Seeking Restoration and Making Amends: Seeking restoration and making amends have far-reaching effects beyond individual relationships. It contributes to the well-being of communities, promotes reconciliation, and demonstrates the transformative power of God's love.

Witnessing to Others: When we actively seek restoration and make amends, we become living testimonies of God's grace and forgiveness. Our actions can inspire others to pursue reconciliation and extend grace.

Building Stronger Communities: The act of seeking restoration and making amends can have a ripple effect, leading to healthier and more harmonious communities. As we take responsibility for our actions and actively work towards reconciliation, we contribute to the healing and restoration of our larger social networks.

Reflecting God's Kingdom: Ultimately, seeking restoration and making amends align with the values of God's Kingdom. In Matthew 5:9, Jesus teaches, "Blessed are the peacemakers, for they shall be called sons of God." By actively seeking restoration, we participate in God's redemptive work, bringing His Kingdom principles to life.

Seeking restoration and making amends are essential elements of the healing and reconciliation process. They require humility, repentance, and a commitment to repairing the harm caused by our actions. Through biblical principles, we are called to actively pursue restoration, reflect God's grace and forgiveness, and contribute to the well-being of individuals and communities. By seeking restoration and making amends, we witness the transformative power of God's love and participate in building a world characterised by reconciliation and healing.

Questions for Reflection

Have I actively sought restoration and made amends with those I have harmed or have been harmed by?

How can I take steps towards reconciliation and healing in those relationships?

Am I willing to take responsibility for my actions and make amends, even if it means going above and beyond what is expected?

How can I demonstrate a genuine commitment to repair the harm caused?

9. Anger Management in Everyday Life

Anger is an emotion that every person experiences at some point. Whether it's a fleeting moment of frustration or a deep-seated resentment, anger can disrupt relationships, hinder personal growth, and even harm our well-being. Managing anger effectively becomes a vital skill that promotes harmony, peace, and healthy emotional well-being in our daily interactions and challenges.

This chapter explores anger management in everyday life, delving into practical strategies and biblical principles that can help us navigate the complexities of anger and harness its energy constructively. By understanding the root causes of anger, developing self-awareness, and adopting healthy coping mechanisms, we can cultivate emotional resilience and transform moments of anger into opportunities for growth and positive change.

The Scriptures provide invaluable guidance and wisdom on handling anger that aligns with God's character and promotes the well-being of ourselves and others. Throughout this chapter, we will draw upon these timeless truths, examining passages that address anger, self-control, and the transformation of our hearts and minds.

As we explore anger management in everyday life, it is important to recognise that anger is not inherently sinful. In fact, the Bible acknowledges that there are righteous forms of anger, such as Jesus' righteous indignation when He confronted injustice. However, our response to anger determines its impact on our lives and relationships.

This chapter will explore practical tips and strategies for managing anger in healthy and constructive ways. We will explore the importance of self-reflection, emotional intelligence, and communication skills in diffusing anger and resolving conflicts. We will address the spiritual dimension of anger management, emphasising the need for prayer, reliance on God's guidance, and transforming our hearts through the power of the Holy Spirit.

Anger management is a lifelong journey that requires ongoing self-reflection, intentional growth, and a willingness to surrender our anger to God's transformative grace. By seeking His wisdom and aligning our thoughts and actions with His teachings, we can cultivate a heart characterised by love, forgiveness, and self-control.

May this chapter serve as a practical and insightful guide for navigating the complexities of anger management in everyday life. May it empower us to respond to anger in ways that honour God, promote healthy relationships, and foster personal growth. May we continually seek His guidance and rely on His strength as we embark on this transformative journey of managing our anger with wisdom and grace.

"Be angry and do not sin; do not let the sun go down on your anger and give no opportunity to the devil" (Ephesians 4:26-27, ESV).

Prayer

Gracious and loving God,

We come before You with humble hearts, recognising the need for Your guidance and wisdom in managing our anger daily. Reflecting on the truths shared in this chapter, we acknowledge that anger is a natural emotion but can become destructive if not handled carefully.

Father, we confess that, at times, our anger has caused harm to ourselves and others. We have allowed it to cloud our judgment, damage relationships, and hinder our witness as Your children. We acknowledge our need for transformation and healing in this area of our lives.

Today, we surrender our anger to You. We lay before You the situations and circumstances that trigger our emotions, knowing You are our refuge and strength. Help us to bring our anger under Your authority, aligning our thoughts and actions with Your will.

Lord, we ask for Your Holy Spirit to fill us with self-control and a spirit of gentleness. Teach us to pause and reflect before reacting in anger, granting us the wisdom to respond with grace and compassion. Show us the power of forgiveness and the importance of seeking reconciliation whenever possible.

In moments of anger, help us to seek solace in Your presence. Remind us of Your love and grace poured out upon us, even when we fall short. May Your peace that surpasses all understanding guard our hearts and minds, keeping us rooted in Your truth.

Father, we pray for the strength to set healthy boundaries and constructively communicate our needs and feelings. Guide our words and actions to reflect Your love and bring about understanding and resolution. Help us to be quick to listen, slow to speak, and slow to become angry, as Your Word instructs us.

Lord, we lift to You those affected by our anger. We ask for Your healing touch upon their hearts and minds. Grant us the humility to seek their forgiveness and the courage to make amends where necessary. May our relationships be restored and strengthened through Your grace.

We also pray for the strength to address the root causes of our anger. Help us recognise and address any underlying hurts, fears, or unresolved conflicts contributing to our emotional reactions. Guide us in seeking professional help or wise counsel if needed so that we may experience true healing and transformation.

Father, we surrender our anger to You, knowing that You are the One who can transform our hearts and minds. Help us to cultivate a spirit of gratitude, kindness, and patience. Empower us to walk in the fruits of the Spirit, reflecting Your character in all we do.

We commit ourselves to daily seeking Your guidance and submitting our emotions to Your loving authority. May our lives testify to Your transformative power as we learn to manage our anger in ways that honour and glorify You.

In Jesus' name, we pray.

Amen.

9.1 Applying Biblical Principles to Daily Challenges

Applying Biblical principles to daily challenges is fundamental to living a life of faith and obedience to God. It involves aligning our thoughts, attitudes, and actions with the teachings and values found in Scripture. By doing so, we can navigate the complexities of life, make wise decisions, and experience God's guidance and blessings. This section will explore the importance of applying Biblical principles to daily challenges and discuss specific areas where these principles can be applied.

The Foundation of Biblical Principles: Biblical principles are derived from the Word of God, which serves as our guide for life. Psalm 119:105 says, "Your word is a lamp to my feet and a light to my path." The Bible provides wisdom, insight, and moral guidance to navigate our challenges. As believers, we must integrate these principles into every aspect of our lives.

Applying Biblical Principles in Daily Challenges: Decision-Making: Every day, we encounter numerous decisions, big and small. Applying Biblical principles helps us make wise choices that align with God's will. Proverbs 3:5-6 reminds us, "Trust in the LORD with all your heart, and do not lean on your understanding. In all your ways, acknowledge him, and he will make straight your paths." By seeking God's guidance through prayer, studying His Word, and seeking wise counsel, we can make decisions that honour God and lead to positive outcomes.

Relationships: Our relationships play a significant role in our daily lives. Applying Biblical principles helps us cultivate healthy and meaningful relationships. For example, Ephesians 4:32 instructs us to "Be kind to one another, tender-hearted, forgiving one another, as God in Christ forgave you." By practising kindness, forgiveness, and love, we create an environment of harmony and unity in our relationships.

Integrity and Ethics: In a world that often compromises ethical standards, applying Biblical principles helps us uphold integrity and moral values. Proverbs 11:3 states, "The integrity of the upright guides them, but the unfaithful are destroyed by their duplicity." By consistently applying principles such as honesty, integrity, and fairness in our daily interactions, we demonstrate our commitment to following Christ's example.

Stewardship: Applying Biblical principles to our resources and responsibilities promotes wise stewardship. Matthew 25:21 reminds us of the importance of being faithful in managing what God has entrusted us: "Well done, good and faithful servant. You have been faithful a little; I will set you over much." By practising generosity, diligence, and responsible management of our time, talents, and finances, we honour God and positively impact others.

Attitude and Mindset: Our attitudes and mindsets greatly influence how we approach daily challenges. Philippians 4:8 advises, "Finally, brothers, whatever is true, whatever is honourable, whatever is just, whatever is pure, whatever is lovely, whatever is commendable if there is any excellence, if there is anything worthy of praise, think about these things." By intentionally focusing our minds on positive, uplifting, and God-honouring thoughts, we cultivate a mindset that enables us to face challenges with faith, hope, and resilience.

Benefits of Applying Biblical Principles: Applying Biblical principles to daily challenges brings numerous benefits to our lives:

Spiritual Growth: By consistently living according to Biblical principles, we grow in our relationship with God and become more Christlike. Colossians 3:10 encourages us, "Put on the new self, which is being renewed in knowledge after the image of its creator." As we apply Biblical principles, our character is transformed, and we reflect the godly virtues and values in our daily lives.

Guidance and Direction: We invite God's guidance and direction when we apply Biblical principles to our daily challenges. Proverbs 16:9 reminds us, "The heart of man plans his way, but the LORD establishes his steps." By aligning our decisions and actions with God's Word, we open ourselves to His leading and experience His faithfulness in guiding us through challenges.

Peace and Contentment: Living by Biblical principles brings peace and contentment to our lives. Isaiah 26:3 assures us, "You keep him in perfect peace whose mind is stayed on you because he trusts in you." We find assurance and tranquillity amidst life's challenges by relying on God's wisdom and following His principles.

Positive Impact on Others: Applying Biblical principles benefits us individually and positively impacts those around us. Matthew 5:16 says, "In the same way, let your light shine before others, so that they may see your good works and give glory to your Father who is in heaven." When we live out Biblical principles daily, we become a testimony to others, inspiring them to seek God's truth and live according to His Word.

Transformation of Society: As individuals consistently apply Biblical principles, the collective impact can lead to the transformation of society. When communities are governed by justice, compassion, and righteousness principles, the result is a society marked by love, unity, and flourishing. Psalm 89:14 affirms, "Righteousness and justice are the foundation of your throne; steadfast love and faithfulness go before you."

Applying Biblical principles to our daily challenges is vital for living a life of faith, obedience, and godly influence. It involves integrating the teachings and values found in Scripture into our decision-making, relationships, integrity, stewardship, and mindset. By doing so, we experience spiritual growth, guidance from God, peace, contentment, and the ability to positively impact others and society. Let us commit ourselves to seeking God's wisdom, studying His Word, and applying

His principles in all aspects of our lives to live as faithful disciples and bearers of His light in the world.

Questions for Reflection

In what areas do I struggle to apply Biblical principles to daily challenges?

How can I intentionally seek God's guidance and align my actions with His Word in those areas?

How can I actively cultivate a mindset focused on truth, purity, and excellence, as encouraged by Philippians 4:8?

What practical steps can I take to renew my mind and align my thoughts with God's principles?

9.2 Transforming Anger into Constructive Action

Anger is a powerful emotion that can positively and negatively affect our lives. Anger can lead to destructive consequences when left uncontrolled or expressed in harmful ways. However, when properly managed and channelled, anger can be transformed into constructive action that brings about positive change and growth. In this section, we will explore how to harness the energy of anger and use it as a catalyst for personal and social transformation, drawing insights from the Bible.

Understanding the Nature of Anger: Before we explore transforming anger into constructive action, it is important to understand the nature of anger. Anger is a natural emotion that arises in response to perceived injustice, mistreatment, or frustration. The Bible acknowledges the existence of anger but cautions against its destructive potential. Ephesians 4:26-27 says, "Be angry and do not sin; do not let the sun go down on your anger, and give no opportunity to the devil." This verse reminds us that anger is not inherently sinful. Still, it should not be allowed to fester and lead us into sinful behaviour.

Self-Reflection and Emotional Awareness: The first step in transforming anger into constructive action is self-reflection and emotional awareness. It involves examining the root causes of our anger, understanding our triggers, and becoming aware of how anger manifests in our thoughts, words, and actions. Proverbs 14:29 teaches us, "Whoever is slow to anger has great understanding, but he who has a hasty temper exalts folly." By developing greater self-awareness, we can gain insight into our anger patterns and respond more thoughtfully and constructively.

Righteous Indignation and Justice: Anger can be a righteous response to injustice and wrongdoing. Jesus exhibited righteous anger when He cleansed the temple in Matthew 21:12-13, overturning the money changers' tables. This demonstrates that anger can serve as a catalyst for standing up against injustice and advocating for righteousness. However, it is crucial to align our anger with God's principles and seek justice in a way that reflects His love and mercy. Proverbs 21:15 reminds us, "When justice is done, it is a joy to the righteous but terror to evildoers." Our anger should be channelled into constructive actions that promote justice and righteousness rather than seeking personal revenge or causing harm.

Seeking Reconciliation and Restoration: Another way to transform anger into constructive action is by seeking reconciliation and restoration. Instead of holding grudges or harbouring resentment, the Bible encourages us to pursue reconciliation and make amends. In Matthew 5:23-24, Jesus instructs, "So if you are offering your gift at the altar and there remember that your brother has something against you, leave your gift there before the altar and go. First, be reconciled to your brother, and then come and offer your gift." This verse emphasises the importance of resolving conflicts and restoring broken relationships. Taking proactive steps towards reconciliation can transform our anger into actions that promote healing and unity.

Advocacy and Social Change: Transforming anger into constructive action also involves channelling our energy towards advocacy and social change. When we see injustice or oppression, our anger can motivate us to speak up, act, and work towards a more just society. Proverbs 31:8-9 encourages us, "Open your mouth for the mute, for the rights of all destitute. Open your mouth, judge righteously, and defend the rights of the poor and needy." By using our voices, resources, and influence to address systemic issues and advocate for the marginalised, we can turn our anger into a force for positive transformation.

Transforming anger into constructive action requires self-reflection, emotional awareness, and a deep commitment to aligning our actions with biblical principles. By recognising the nature of anger, embracing righteous indignation, seeking reconciliation, and advocating for social change, we can harness the energy of anger and use it as a catalyst for personal growth and positive transformation.

The Bible provides wisdom, guidance, and examples of navigating and transforming our anger. Through prayer, seeking divine wisdom, and studying relevant biblical passages, we can better understand God's perspective on anger and learn how to respond in ways honouring Him.

As we apply biblical principles to our daily challenges, we can experience greater self-control, forgiveness, humility, patience, love, and compassion. Our relationships can be healed and restored, and we can become agents of change in our communities and society.

Ultimately, transforming anger into constructive action requires reliance on God and His transformative power. By surrendering our anger to Him, trusting in His plan and sovereignty, and seeking His guidance, we can develop resilience, overcome anger through faith, and experience true healing and transformation.

May we cultivate a lifestyle of peace, self-control, and righteous action guided by the principles found in God's Word. Let us continually reflect on these teachings and allow them to shape our hearts, minds, and actions as we navigate the complexities of anger and strive to become more Christ-like in all our lives.

Questions for Reflection

How can I better align my anger with God's principles and use it to catalyse positive change in my life and others?

How can I seek reconciliation, make amends, and promote justice in my relationships and community, even when challenging?

9.3 Developing a Lifestyle of Peace and Self-control

Developing a lifestyle of peace and self-control is vital to anger management and personal growth. It requires intentional choices, a transformed mindset, and a reliance on God's strength to overcome our natural inclinations towards anger and hostility. This section will explore the biblical teachings and principles that guide us in cultivating peace and self-control.

Peace, both inner peace and peace with others, is a recurring theme throughout the Bible. Jesus, our ultimate example, spoke extensively about peace and encouraged His followers to be peacemakers. In the Beatitudes, He declared, "Blessed are the peacemakers, for they will be called children of God" (Matthew 5:9). Jesus Himself embodied peace, and He offers us His peace as a gift: "Peace I leave with you; my peace I give you. I do not give to you as the world gives. Do not let your hearts be troubled and do not be afraid" (John 14:27).

To develop a lifestyle of peace, we must first seek peace within ourselves. This begins with surrendering our worries, fears, and anxieties to God. The Apostle Paul reminds us, "Do not be anxious about anything, but in every situation, by prayer and petition, with thanksgiving, present your requests to God. And the peace of God, which transcends all understanding, will guard your hearts and your minds in Christ Jesus" (Philippians 4:6-7). By entrusting our concerns to God and relying on His peace, we can experience inner tranquillity even in challenging circumstances.

Cultivating peace involves nurturing healthy relationships with others. The Bible encourages us to pursue peace with everyone and to live in harmony. Romans 12:18 advises, "If it is possible, as far as it depends on you, live at peace with everyone." This requires humility, forgiveness, and a commitment to resolving conflicts constructively.

Jesus teaches us in Matthew 5:23-24 that before presenting our offerings to God, we should seek reconciliation with anyone we have offended or who has something against us. This shows the importance of prioritising peace in our relationships and seeking forgiveness and reconciliation when necessary.

Self-control is another crucial aspect of developing a lifestyle of peace. It is closely connected to managing our emotions and responses, including anger. The Apostle Paul lists self-control as one of the fruits of the Spirit in Galatians 5:22-23, highlighting its significance in the life of a believer. Self-control involves discipline, restraint, and a conscious effort to align our actions with God's will. It requires surrendering our impulses to the Holy Spirit and allowing Him to guide our thoughts, words, and behaviours.

The Bible offers practical guidance on developing self-control. Proverbs 25:28 warns, "Like a city whose walls are broken through is a person who lacks self-control." This metaphor emphasises the importance of maintaining boundaries and guarding against impulsive reactions. Proverbs 16:32 states, "Better a patient person than a warrior, one with self-control than one who takes a city." This verse highlights the strength and wisdom of exercising self-control rather than succumbing to anger and aggression.

Developing self-control also involves renewing our minds and aligning our thoughts with God's truth. The Apostle Paul encourages believers in Romans 12:2, "Do not conform to the pattern of this world but be transformed by renewing your mind. Then you can test and approve God's will—his good, pleasing and perfect will." By immersing ourselves in God's Word and allowing His truth to shape our thinking, we can develop a mindset rooted in peace, self-control, and godly wisdom.

Practising self-control and cultivating a lifestyle of peace requires consistent effort and reliance on God's grace. It is not something that happens overnight but is a lifelong journey of growth and transformation. As we abide in Christ and allow the Holy Spirit to work in us, we can experience the fruit of self-control and peace manifesting in our lives.

Living a life of peace and self-control also extends beyond our personal interactions. It involves how we engage with the world around us, including our response to challenging situations, conflicts, and injustices. The Bible calls us to pursue justice and righteousness while maintaining peace and self-control.

Micah 6:8 guides us on conducting ourselves: "He has shown you, O mortal, what is good. And what does the LORD require of you? Act justly, love mercy, and walk humbly with your God." This verse reminds us that seeking justice should be coupled with love and humility. Even in the face of injustice, we are called to respond with grace and self-control, following the example of Jesus.

As we develop a lifestyle of peace and self-control, we become agents of reconciliation and instruments of God's love in a broken world. Our transformed lives testify to the power of God's grace and the work of the Holy Spirit within us. We can influence others by our example, demonstrating the peace and self-control that flows from a deep relationship with God.

Developing a lifestyle of peace and self-control is a journey that requires intentional choices, dependence on God, and a commitment to aligning our lives with biblical principles. Through prayer, surrender, and the guidance of the Holy Spirit, we can experience inner peace and exhibit self-control in our thoughts, words, and actions. This benefits our personal well-being and impacts our relationships and interactions with others. As we navigate daily challenges, conflicts, and growth opportunities, let us strive to live out the teachings of Scripture, allowing the peace of God to rule in our hearts and being guided by the Spirit to exercise self-control. By doing so, we reflect the character of Christ and contribute to a more peaceful and harmonious world.

May Psalm 34:14 constantly remind us: "Turn from evil and do good; seek peace and pursue it." Let us pursue peace and self-control as we walk with God and seek to bring His light and love to the world around us.

Questions for Reflection

How can I actively cultivate peace and self-control in my daily life?

What areas of my life require greater self-control and a deeper commitment to peace, and how can I seek God's guidance in those areas?

10. Conclusion

10.1 Summary of Key Biblical Teachings on Anger Management

Anger is a powerful emotion that, if not managed properly, can have destructive consequences in our lives and relationships. Throughout the Bible, we find key teachings and principles that guide how to manage anger healthily and godly. This section will summarise some of these key biblical teachings on anger management.

Recognising the Root Causes of Anger: Anger often stems from deeper issues such as pride, unmet expectations, injustice, or wounded emotions. The Bible encourages us to examine the root causes of our anger and address them with wisdom and discernment.

Proverbs 14:29 says, "Whoever is slow to anger has great understanding, but he who has a hasty temper exalts folly." This verse highlights the importance of understanding the underlying reasons for our anger and exercising self-control.

Practising Self-Control: The Bible emphasises the importance of self-control in managing anger. It teaches us to be slow to anger and to respond with measured and thoughtful actions.

Proverbs 16:32 states, "Whoever is slow to anger is better than the mighty, and he who rules his spirit than he who takes a city." This verse highlights the strength of self-control and its superiority over giving in to anger.

Seeking Reconciliation and Forgiveness: Anger can damage relationships and hinder reconciliation. The Bible encourages us to seek forgiveness and reconciliation from God and others.

Ephesians 4:26-27 says, "Be angry and do not sin; do not let the sun go down on your anger and give no opportunity to the devil." This verse reminds us to address our anger promptly and seek resolution, preventing it from festering and causing further harm.

Responding with Love and Kindness: Instead of reacting in anger, the Bible teaches us to respond with love, kindness, and compassion. It encourages us to overcome evil with good.

Proverbs 15:1 states, "A soft answer turns away wrath, but a harsh word stirs up anger." This verse highlights the power of gentle and kind responses in diffusing anger and promoting peace.

Seeking God's Help and Guidance: Recognising our own limitations, the Bible urges us to seek God's help in managing anger. Through prayer, surrender, and reliance on the Holy Spirit, we can find the strength and wisdom to overcome anger and respond in ways honouring God.

James 1:19-20 advises, "Know this, my beloved brothers: let every person be quick to hear, slow to speak, slow to anger; for the anger of man does not produce the righteousness of God." This passage emphasises the importance of listening, self-restraint and seeking God's righteousness instead of allowing anger to control us.

The Bible provides us with valuable guidance and teachings on anger management. It emphasises the importance of self-control, understanding the root causes of anger, seeking reconciliation and forgiveness, responding with love and kindness, and relying on God for help and guidance. By incorporating these principles into our lives, we can navigate the challenges of anger in a way that promotes peace, strengthens relationships, and reflects the character of Christ.

It is important to remember that anger itself is not inherently sinful, as there are instances where righteous anger can be appropriate. However, the Bible encourages us to manage our anger to align with God's principles without letting it lead us to sin or harm others.

By examining our hearts and seeking God's grace and transformation, we can grow in our ability to manage anger to bring glory to God and promote love, peace, and reconciliation in our lives and relationships. May we continually rely on the Holy Spirit to guide and empower us in our journey towards anger management rooted in biblical principles.

10.2 Encouragement for Personal Growth and Transformation

Personal growth and transformation are essential aspects of our journey as believers. As we strive to manage our anger following biblical principles, the Bible offers us encouragement and guidance for our ongoing development. Through the transformative power of God's Word and the work of the Holy Spirit in our lives, we can experience growth, healing, and transformation.

Embracing God's Grace and Forgiveness: One of the key aspects of personal growth and transformation is understanding and embracing God's grace and forgiveness. The Bible reminds us that we have all fallen short of God's standards (Romans 3:23), and yet, through the sacrifice of Jesus Christ, we have received forgiveness and redemption (Ephesians 1:7). This awareness of God's unconditional love and forgiveness enables us to extend the same grace and forgiveness to others, including ourselves, as we navigate the challenges of anger management.

Reflection questions:

- How can I fully embrace and live in the reality of God's grace and forgiveness in my life?
- How can I extend grace and forgiveness to those who have hurt or angered me?

Cultivating a Spirit of Humility: Humility is a vital character trait contributing to our personal growth and transformation. The Bible repeatedly emphasises the value of humility before God and others (Proverbs 11:2, James 4:6). By recognising our weaknesses and limitations, we can develop a humble attitude that allows us to learn from our mistakes, seek reconciliation, and grow in wisdom and maturity.

Reflection questions:

- How can I cultivate a spirit of humility in my interactions with others, especially when anger rises?
- What steps can I take to humbly seek reconciliation and admit my faults when my anger has caused harm in my relationships?

Surrendering Control to God: Personal growth and transformation require surrendering control and allowing Him to work in and through us. The Bible teaches us to trust the Lord with all our hearts and lean not on our understanding (Proverbs 3:5-6). Regarding anger management, we must recognise that true transformation comes from the Holy Spirit's work within us. Through the power of God, we can overcome anger and develop a lifestyle marked by peace, self-control, and love.

Reflection questions:

- In what areas do I struggle to surrender control to God, including managing my anger?
- How can I invite the Holy Spirit daily to lead and guide my anger management journey and personal growth?

Practising Daily Renewal: Personal growth and transformation require consistent effort and intentional practices. The Bible encourages us to renew our minds and be transformed by renewing our minds (Romans 12:2). This renewal takes place through regular engagement with God's Word, prayer, and fellowship with other believers. By immersing ourselves in the truth of God's Word and surrounding ourselves with a supportive community, we can experience ongoing growth and transformation in managing our anger.

Reflection questions:

- How can I prioritise daily engagement with God's Word and prayer to renew my mind and grow my ability to manage anger?
- Am I actively seeking accountability and support from fellow believers to foster personal growth and transformation in anger management?

Embracing the Journey of Growth: Finally, personal growth and transformation in anger management are ongoing processes. We must approach this journey with patience, perseverance, and a willingness to learn from our experiences. The Bible assures us that God, who began a good work in us, will continue until the day of Christ Jesus (Philippians 1:6).

Reflection questions:

- How am I actively embracing and living in the reality of God's grace and forgiveness in my life? In what ways can I extend that grace and forgiveness to others?
- How can I cultivate a spirit of humility in my interactions, especially when anger arises? What steps can I take to humbly seek reconciliation and admit my faults when my anger has caused harm in my relationships?
- In what areas do I struggle to surrender control to God, including managing my anger? How can I invite the Holy Spirit daily to lead and guide my anger management journey and personal growth?
- How can I prioritise daily engagement with God's Word and

prayer to renew my mind and grow my ability to manage anger? Am I actively seeking accountability and support from fellow believers to foster personal growth and transformation in anger management?

- How do I view the journey of growth in managing anger? Am I embracing it with patience, perseverance, and a willingness to learn from my experiences? How can I continue to seek God's guidance and rely on His strength to grow and transform in this area of my life?

- Are there specific triggers or patterns of behaviour that I need to address in my journey of anger management and personal growth? How can I proactively respond to those triggers and replace negative patterns with healthier responses guided by biblical principles?

- How can I actively incorporate the fruit of the Spirit, including love, joy, peace, patience, kindness, goodness, faithfulness, gentleness, and self-control, into my daily life? What practical steps can I take to cultivate these qualities and allow them to influence my interactions and responses to anger-inducing situations?

- How can I express gratitude and praise to God for my progress in managing my anger? How can I celebrate the small victories and acknowledge His faithfulness in transforming my heart and behaviour?

- Am I open to seeking professional help or counselling if needed to support my journey of anger management and personal growth? How can I humbly and courageously reach out for assistance and utilise the resources available to me to pursue emotional and spiritual well-being?

- How can I actively share my experiences and the lessons I have learned in managing anger with others? How can I be a source of encouragement and support to those struggling in this area, pointing them towards the transformative power of God's Word and the hope of personal growth and healing?

Regularly engaging in personal reflection and honestly exploring these questions can deepen our understanding of ourselves, strengthen our relationship with God, and continue to grow in anger management and personal transformation.

Final Prayer

Gracious and loving God,

We come before You with hearts filled with gratitude for the journey we have embarked upon through this book. We thank You for the wisdom and guidance You have imparted to us as we have explored the depths of our emotions, examined the teachings of Your Word, and sought to align our lives with Your will.

Reflecting on our lessons, we recognise that true transformation and growth can only come through Your grace and power. We acknowledge that we wholly depend on You and surrender ourselves again into Your loving hands.

Thank You for opening our eyes to the consequences of uncontrolled anger and reminding us of the need to seek Your guidance in managing our emotions. Thank You for illuminating our path's biblical principles revealing Your heart for reconciliation, forgiveness, and grace.

We are grateful for the lessons about humility, meekness, and the power of a transformed heart. Thank You for reminding us of the importance of self-reflection, responsibility, and seeking reconciliation in our relationships.

Lord, as we conclude this journey, we commit ourselves to continually seeking Your wisdom, grace, and strength. Help us to apply the principles we have learned in practical ways, not only in our interactions with others but also in our daily lives. May our words and actions reflect Your love, mercy, and compassion.

We pray for the courage to extend forgiveness, the willingness to seek reconciliation, and the humility to make amends where necessary. Guide us in building relationships marked by grace, understanding, and effective communication. Use us as instruments of peace and agents of healing in a world often torn apart by anger and strife.

Father, we ask for Your guidance in navigating the challenges of everyday life. Grant us the patience and long-suffering to endure hardships with faith and perseverance. Teach us to surrender to Your will and to trust in Your plan and sovereignty.

Lord, we pray for the transformation of our hearts to become vessels of Your grace and forgiveness. Help us to reflect Your character in all we do, extending love, compassion, and understanding to those around us.

Finally, we thank You for Your faithfulness throughout this journey. We acknowledge that only by Your Spirit working within us can we truly overcome anger, experience healing and reconciliation, and grow into the likeness of Christ.

May the lessons learned in this book be etched into our hearts and minds, guiding our thoughts, words, and actions. Empower us to be ambassadors of Your love and agents of change in a world in desperate need of Your grace.

We offer this prayer in the name of Jesus, our Savior and Redeemer. Amen.

About the Author

Andrew Lamont-Turner is a theological scholar, author, and Bible teacher who has dedicated his life to pursuing theological knowledge and disseminating spiritual wisdom. With a profound understanding of the scriptures and a passion for teaching, Andrew has emerged as a leading voice in the field of theology. His extensive academic qualifications and love for God and his family have shaped him into a multifaceted individual committed to nurturing spiritual growth and intellectual exploration.

Academic Journey: Andrew's academic journey reflects his thirst for theological understanding. He holds a Bachelor of Theology, Bachelor of Theology (Honours), Master of Theology, and a Doctor of Philosophy in Theology. These qualifications represent years of rigorous study and a commitment to excellence in his field. Furthermore, Andrew's intellectual curiosity extends beyond theology, as he also possesses a Bachelor of Education (Honours) and several Postgraduate Certificates in various commercial fields. This interdisciplinary approach has enriched his perspective and broadened his ability to connect theological principles with everyday life.

Teaching and Writing: Andrew's knowledge of theology has been expressed through his teaching and writing endeavours. As an educator, he has inspired countless students through his engaging lectures and insights into the scriptures. His ability to distil complex theological concepts into accessible teachings has garnered him a reputation as an exceptional communicator.

In addition to his teaching, Andrew is a prolific author who has published several books and a comprehensive Bible study series. His books delve into various aspects of Christian theology, offering insights, practical guidance, and thought-provoking reflections. With meticulous research, clear exposition, and a genuine desire to bridge the gap between academic theology and everyday faith, Andrew's writings have touched the lives of many, nurturing their spiritual growth and deepening their understanding of God's Word.

Pastoral Leadership: Living his faith ensures Andrew takes his Pastoral Leadership very seriously. He is the Pastor of a community church in rural South Africa, where he ensures the flock entrusted to him by God is well-fed and looked after.

Read more at https://ncts.education/nctseminary/course/view.php?id=25.